# *Leave Me a Line*

## *A Memoir*

**Lenny Gill**

# Dedication

This book is dedicated to my wife Pat and my lovely children and grandchildren. It is also dedicated to my parents and grandparents and to the countless generations before them who have lived and died unremarked, and are remembered now only in official records.

My thanks also go to Gill Chilton who has provided me with invaluable stylistic advice and editing.

"You are a very fine person, Mr. Baggins, and I am very fond of you; but you are only quite a little fellow in a wide world after all!"

(The Hobbit by J.R.R. Tolkien 1937)

# Table of Contents

'It's a dangerous business, going
out of your door!'

# 'Look on my Works, ye Mighty, and despair!'

('Ozymandias' – Percy Bysshe Shelley)

## Day One

Whoosh! I am engulfed in sheeting flame – where did that come from?

I am locked into the line to left and right, and my shield moves forward alone, along with its fellows as I let go of the handles and leap back away from the sudden flame.

At first, I don't notice the pain, even though it has seared deep into my arm between glove and tunic. I use my other arm to brush away what I realise is the smouldering cloth of my jacket and jump back to retrieve my shield handles and re-join the line as we inch carefully forward.

The above could be a description of medieval knights locked in battle. But no! It is 1981, and I am one of hundreds of police officers on the street in Liverpool. We are carrying interlocking plastic shields that form a continuous line across Upper Parliament street in the south end of Liverpool. We are less than a mile away from the city's main shopping centre and just 800 yards from our own Headquarters. And we are under attack from a hostile crowd that sees us - me, as their enemy.

Suddenly, I am the end man in our line as Brian, to my left, is engulfed in flame. He drops his shield, my shield unlocks. He jumps back falling to the ground, rolling to extinguish his flaming jacket and passes from my line of sight.

# The smell of petrol

A trap has been set. Petrol has been poured into a shallow metal oven tray looted from the nearby school kitchen and laid in a line of its many fellows across the road. As we step on the tray, unable to see, we cower and stumble blindly forward behind our already opaque riot shields protecting our bent forms from helmet tip to boot, a petrol bomb is hurled at our feet. The fuel we are now standing in engulfs us, forcing the line to skip and dance forward, leaving the flaming trays in our wake. It takes all our effort to keep the shields locked and maintain our precarious protection as flames lick at our heels.

By this time I am at the junction with Grove Street, which leads away into stygian darkness to my left. It is mercifully free of 'hostiles' as my left is now exposed. They have retreated before us, having smashed the street lamps in their wake so now I am edging forward, shoulder to shoulder with more than 120 of my colleagues in three huddled, fearful lines. The darkness is lit only by blazing cars, petrol bombs and traps like the one I have just walked into.

Hurtling towards us in the dark and at the edge of sight are cars. Their skidding wheels smoke, as rubber burns; their engines scream as the drivers (only a few of whom are over 15) demonstrate their impunity, and we (normally the predators ourselves) are forced to keep our heads down to avoid their missiles.

Barely six hours pass, but it feels like it could've been days. The light of day takes hold, revealing the carnage before us. We are suddenly very cold, shivering in the dawn as the street clears of belligerents.

A fresh colleague – from Lancashire I think or maybe even far off Cumbria – taps my shoulder to tell me I am relieved for the time being, and can go to the rear. I and my mates stumble our exhausted, dazed way back to a personnel carrier and from there to the Police Station just under two miles (and a thousand years) away to be patched up, debriefed and briefly sent home to reassure our loved ones that we're still alive. We get four hours' sleep before we are expected to be back to the fray.

I wonder to myself, Is this the revolution that my Dad always said would happen? It certainly seemed like it to me during that endless week of violence.

By the time we trudged away, 120 men had been reduced to less than a dozen, the rest in hospital with burns or missile injuries. What remained of our line was more than 200 yards behind where we had begun that long night. Our starting point was marked by a blazing warehouse. It wasn't the shields that saved us, nor our meagre equipment, but a spontaneous decision by those of us left to throw bricks back at the rioters – the only thing that did the trick and drove them back in the end

https://www.youtube.com/watch?v=LVW1T-Blhfg

### Day Two

Hum! Clink! Chink! An electric whirr reverberates through the air as milk floats carry a deadly cargo toward us.

Dozens of petrol-filled milk bottles are neatly stacked in their crates. These electric dodgems, which were stolen from the depot a few hours previously, are now able to cause serious damage. Our frenzied adversaries are back and have set these bottles ablaze and jammed a brick against the pedal of the accelerating milk floats towards our line. We wait, refreshed once more by our four-hour sleep and reinforced with patched up colleagues or additions shipped in from further afield.

### Anarchy. Thuggery. Revolution

It started on 4th July 1981. I am a 24-year-old constable with Merseyside Police. I have a wife and a young baby staying with my mother-in-law, Nanny Mac, for safety. As the petrol bombs fly toward us, I wonder whether I will ever see Pat or baby Lenny again.

'Stand your ground,' is the order. And we do, forming a human barrier like a latter-day British Waterloo square, determined we will not let the rioters break through our line. Despite our efforts, like our forefathers at Abu Klea during the Sudan Campaign of 1885, our square is broken.

At Abu Klea, defeat sent shudders of disbelief through the British government, but here in Toxteth, only an assistant chief constable stands in our midst and looks just lost and out of his depth, his world and certainty dissolving before his eyes. I had more immediate problems.

Standing my ground is not easy. Now and again, we make a baton charge toward the angry crowd, who are screaming and laughing. Throwing missiles at us. They run back temporarily, unencumbered as we are with shield and heavy woollen uniform in this stifling summer night, but they always come back and batter us once more.

Incredibly, in 1981, we have no specialist equipment. We wear our regular serge uniform. Days later, we will be advised to go into sports shops and buy shin pads and cricket boxes at our own expense. I will wear my motorcycle helmet with POLICE painted on it and count myself lucky that I have one.

Someone remembers some metal shields dating back to 1919, when the police faced mobs of angry strikers. These old, battered shields have been  languishing in a stock room at the Pier Head for more than 60 years, all through the blitz and beyond and have been long since forgotten but incredibly they still work and are a damn-site more effective than the plastic things we have now, too long, too unwieldy and more of a hindrance than a help. Months later, surplus helmets and short shields will arrive from the army in Belfast, but by then, it'll be a little too late.

Yet none of this equipment is there during those first, brutal days. Our high, domed police helmets are made from papier-mache, and we are issued a thin Perspex visor attached to the paper helmet with an elastic band. They are no match for the bricks that are hurled at us. When a sharpened metal railing is thrown at one bobbie's head, it goes straight through his helmet, and he wears a steel plate in his skull for the rest of his life.

For the last few days of the riots, I take on the role of first-aider, ironic perhaps, as I ignored my own injury. But then there is bravery all around me. Officers falling to the ground and then getting up and carrying on. Whenever an officer does go down and is so injured, he is unable to stand, I drag him to safety behind a wall, or if there is no wall in near reach, behind a police vehicle. I apply dressings and plastic skin I have liberated from A & E. I do the best I can. It has the added advantage that I can take a short breather into the bargain.

On one of the later days of the riots, the line is assailed by a new threat at the corner of Kingsley Road. The rioters have attacked and ransacked a fire station, and a stolen fire engine bears down on our steadfast square. As it trundles slowly but relentlessly through the line and comes to rest against an abandoned van, the line disintegrates, and several officers fall injured, rioters surging forward and into contact.

I run out among the rioters to rescue a seriously injured colleague and throw him unceremoniously into the back of a marked Sherpa van; I bang on the bulkhead and shout 'Go!' Only there is no driver.

I truly believed the mob were going to kill me. These people think nothing of upturning vans, and of setting them alight.

Fortunately I spotted an officer I knew who had driven a van to the site earlier that day and might now have the keys to this van. He did, jumped in and took the wheel before we were overwhelmed. Just minutes later we got to the Royal Hospital, which looked for all the world like the war zones I would see many years later in the third world, and after a half-hour breather, I returned to the front line (rather reluctantly I must admit).

Twelve hours later, it was light once more. The mob was at last sated, and I could go back to my family for another four-hour kip before it all started again.

July 1981 went on like this night after night before finally petering out after almost a month of havoc and exhaustion.

Later, my commanding officer told me my actions had been recommended for a George Medal. Yet the government had deemed it inappropriate, to publicly recognise police officers when tensions within minority communities remained fragile. Instead, I was promoted. That would do, I thought.

The Toxteth riots were part of a summer of violence that happened in every major city in England which were presented to the wider world as the local community's response to what it perceived to be heavy-handed policing, particularly towards young black men. Maybe they were at least partly right, but the bigger picture was the debilitating effect of living in an inner-city area with unacceptable levels of unemployment and the behind-the-scenes influence of organised criminals intent on emasculating the police response to their crimes.

What I saw wasn't the peaceful, lawful actions of those who believe themselves to be genuinely oppressed. What began as a protest against police powers by a few people was quickly hijacked by criminals who utilised the chaos of the situation to introduce physical violence and to loot from shops and houses. It was the hottest, driest July in years. Tempers rose with the temperature. On streets throughout the cities of the UK, cars and buildings were set ablaze. House and shop windows were smashed, and people were terrorised.

For ten exhausting days, the Operational Support Division, Merseyside Police's elite unit – of which I was a proud part – did not give in. We had practically no rest. We had no time to write records in our notebooks. We were brought food and drink sporadically by the Salvation Army. Police from other forces – as far away as Devon – joined in. Around five hundred officers were seriously injured in Liverpool alone, many with what are now euphemistically called 'life-changing injuries', both mental and physical, from which some never really recovered.

All the other vital work that police do – protecting the vulnerable, responding to emergency calls, preventing serious crime – it all carried on just the same, undertaken by officers long past their operational best in the majority of cases. Everything we did to stem the riots was work on top.

The riots ended when, at last, after those ten days, God's Policeman came to our aid . . . it rained. Central government in the guise of Michael Heseltine announced an enhanced support programme for Toxteth. Tensions that always rise in hot weather ebbed away in the rain, and at last, peace returned to our streets. On 28th July 1981, the riots were over. No winners. But I had survived. I went home, hugged and kissed my wife and held my son.

It's the acrid smell and the noise that, to this day, I remember, as well as the fear, uncertainty and yes, the adrenaline rush. But no situation is without the absurd and, after all these years, two images are with me still. The first is of a policeman nearing retirement and clearly long past his best stuffed into a uniform he had not worn since he had begun his day job years before – the uniform of the Liverpool City Police, disbanded fourteen years before. The second is bizarre.

As our square was assailed by fire and missiles, as sirens screamed and destruction reigned, my attention was drawn to a man who could have been my own father, standing on a chair, just twenty yards away from the exploding petrol bombs calmly painting the windows of his council house, seemingly oblivious to the mayhem around him. Such were the Toxteth riots of 1981: the summer of discontent.

I am not generally one for reflection. Some accuse me of lacking emotion, at times. I try to weigh up decisions with care, act accordingly and decisively and then move on to the next set of tasks. Once the dust had settled on the Toxteth riots, I knew I wanted to write about how it felt to have lived through them. Then I got to thinking about the rest of my police career. So much has happened that I wanted to set it all down. In retirement now, finally, I have the time to do so. It helps, when it comes to thinking about reflection, to have a milestone birthday to act as an anchor point. I turned 65 this year.

Tracing my ancestry is important to me – and with that comes the responsibility of ensuring my own life is documented also. For my memoir, I knew that I wanted the emphasis to be my career and my family. And with that has come also a degree of necessary, and surprisingly rewarding, reflection.

11

I feel fortunate to have done well, or at least reasonably so. In my life, I have achieved almost all I could have wished for, and in some cases, more: reasonable career progression, a large (and I think generally well adjusted) and loving family and a country pile without the daily bother of aggravation or neighbours. I prefer animals to people as neighbours on the whole.

I am the boy who started out in a tiny cottage in Etna Street and then a barely larger flat above a chip shop in Kirkby new town who can now look out of the farmhouse he owns in rural Wales and see the hills all around, the sheep grazing and apples ripening in his own small orchard. I have a reasonable pension to support my wife and I. We who have been together a lifetime and hope to be together for many more years to come.

As a senior officer during most of my 30 years of police service and a further decade as an international consultant for humanitarian organisations, I have I think changed and saved lives. I have also seen close up the very worst in people who act horrifically under domestic duress or who become criminals, sadists and terrorists.

As well as standing my ground against the rioters in Toxteth, I have been yards away from a tank fight in Sudan and even closer to Islamic extremists in Pakistan, Libya and Gaza. Yet all of this pales beside one night in a Premier Inn in Sheffield, when my ability to act quickly, unemotionally and without panic saved my wife's life. But more about Pat, my six children and – currently – twelve grandchildren later. They know already that they are my world, and without them, my life would be a hollow shell.

# Leave Me a Line

This is my book's chosen title. The phrase may leap out at those of a certain age with police experience. For everyone else – here's the reason for such an odd title.

In my first posting as a young constable on the beat in Huyton, keeping my notebook up to date was vital and failure to do so punished heavily. Twice each day, the sergeant would read my entries and then sign them off. Typically, I'd jot down addresses visited, information gathered, and circumstances of arrests and summonses issued (we called it process). But sometimes, I would be too busy or lazy perhaps.

As Barliman Butterbur, the owner of The Prancing Pony in The Lord of the Rings, often says, 'One thing drives out another.' Policing is a job like no other: if you're chasing a suspect or helping a person in distress, you can't always stop what you're doing to get out your pencil.

'Leave me a line,' the sergeant would say for instances like this, with a gap where his signature entry should be, and he would sign it at the end of the shift when the entries were complete. And so it is with this book: it is a record of events, largely in the correct order and brought to full life as I share the stories that underpin them. Pulling together these key moments and bringing out the personalities of the people who have shared them with me has been a satisfying process.

There is some high drama and tension, some successes and setbacks. There is also, I hope, love and good humour, plus a little Merseyside quirkiness of course! I feel very fortunate with what I have achieved and experienced. Do join me as I journey through the years. And if you remember something I haven't – just leave me a line! I have so much I still intend to do in life . . . any extra recollections could just find their way into Volume Two!

Lenny Gill
Summer 2022.

# Memory or Myth

> ## 'The past is a foreign country; they do things differently there.'
> (L. P. Hartley – 'The Go-Between')

Edward Gill, my grandad, Ted, was a nice man, though straight upright and stern at times.

He always had a bad chest which was made much much worse by smoking ten Players Navy-Cut cigarettes a day, then probably the strongest cigarettes on sale.

He had a bad chest and so had his father who blamed it on his work in the Old Swan Borax factory, Borax was a chemical used in soap making apparently. Ted's bad chest passed to my dad, who blamed it on smoking and he has passed it down to me though I blame it on being too fat. Whatever the cause the family bad chest remains.

Anyway my Grandad's bad chest, caused him to spit in the open fire, disgusting habit I know but in fairness he couldn't help it. Spitting was a big problem generally, so much so that there were public signs prohibiting spitting and carrying a big fine to prevent the spread of Tuberculosis (TB) which was rife until the mid 1960s.

**I digress.**

Unfortunately when we lived in the Prefab in Huyton we didn't have an open fire but a new fangled 2 bar electric fire with a coal effect lit by an orange 40 watt bulb. One day Grandad came to visit. To my mums extreme dismay and annoyance, he spat in the fire not once but several times. I can't remember him visiting much after that.

He was otherwise a healthy man, over 6 feet and spare but not thin. Apart from the chest business he was always in fine fettle until that is he reached his seventieth birthday. Then he caught Shingles (a form of chicken pox but without the spots which causes blisters and extreme pain to the nerves).

From my vantage point today I realise he must have been in enormous pain. He sat in his chair, occasionally spitting in the fire and playing draughts with me but took to holding his side which must have been badly blistered and very painful. Unfortunately in the ignorance and cruelty of youth, egged on by my dad who never really got on with his father after he married mum who was a catholic (more of that later), we called the poor man Napoleon, a moniker which lasted until his death just four years later. Such mockery was cruel and ignorant of us, but give him his due he always took it in good part.

One day when he came in from work. He was a Tram driver in the 1950s and in my day a bus driver plying the numbers 9 and 10 routes

from Green Lane depot to Huyton. I asked him, *'Was anyone in our family killed in the Second World War?'*

*'No, son,'* he said and nothing more, in his Liverpudlian accent which was nothing like the Scouse accent of today, (I have attached a link below to YouTube so you can hear the Liverpool accent as it was in the 1960s.) .

**https://www.youtube.com/watch?v=rb8L4JHUgtw**

Grandad was born in 1902 and he'd been too young to fight in the First World War. Then he'd been too old for call-up in the next one. He was instead a Police Special Constable. But Grandad was one of eleven children, as coincidentally was my nan Lilly. What of all these brothers and sisters? Could all twenty two have been unscathed by the wars? They wouldn't say but I got the impression that had been the case.

Many years later and due to my persistent interest in genealogy I discovered one of my mother's older brothers was killed, and two of Grandad Gill's brothers were killed, in the war. One died from an illness whilst on active service, the other on a troop ship torpedoed off the coast of Sierra Leone. One of them actually left his mother – Catherine, my great-grandmother – a considerable sum of money. I have a copy of the War Office telegram sent to Catherine, informing her of her son's death and a copy of the will leaving the money.

But none of it was ever mentioned, even when prompted. Odd.

Like the fact that my dad himself was born two months after his parents married in 1926. Things happened; the Gills, hard-working,

19

companionable people that they were, just got on with their lot and
rarely it seemed, dwelled on the past.

Emotions were never spoken about either. Conversation, when it
did happen, centred on the mechanics of daily living. What time
would my nan be home from her laundry job in Derwent Road off
Green Lane? What was for tea?

In that way, and in
that way alone, as it
turns out, they met
their match in my
mum's family. My
mother's father,
Leonard Miller, who
died before I was
born, worked as a
carter. In 1942, he
received a bravery
award and medal
from the Shipwreck
and Humane Society
of Liverpool for
assisting a
policeman stopping
a runaway horse.

Again – never mentioned. I only found out myself about 3 years
ago looking in the archives, otherwise I would still be ignorant.

20

Retrospectively proud when I made the discovery I arranged a replica of the award certificate and presented it to his daughter, my Aunty Theresa. My own mum, Bridie, had already died. But Theresa was still thriving in her late 80s. *'Oh, thank you, Len,'* she said. *'That's the best present I've ever had'* Then she disappeared upstairs – returning with the original certificate! She'd known all about her father's act of bravery, but like so much good, middling and bad in both sides of the family, it was left unsaid – or muddled up to resemble more myth than memory.

Mum's family black sheep was one Edward Millichip (1839–1920), my great-great-grandfather. In February 1880, Edward was convicted of manslaughter following a fatal fight the previous December with a man he'd been drinking with at the Great Eastern Pub in Langdale Street, Liverpool. He was sentenced to 20 years, serving the sentence first at HM Chatham and then at HM Dartmoor. The man survived, and on his release lived out his remaining two decades back in Liverpool, actually just five houses away from his grandchildren, my own grandparents. No-one mentioned it (or him) and when I found out and probed, they seemed simply disinterested and denied knowledge.

The tale of Edward and his moment of violent madness is a tragic one. His wife Julia had five children before his incarceration. Julia died in the Liverpool workhouse and all but one of her children died before they were forty. It is a tale of poverty and a descent into petty crime worthy of Dickens. Despite the last child Emma surviving, marrying my Great Grandfather Miller and turning her life around to become one of the worthy poor, mum and her family said nothing and never alluded to the skeletons in the family cupboard. Had it not been for Emma I, and you dear reader would not be here. Do you

## KICKING A MAN TO DEATH.

Edward Millichip, alias Ashcroft, aged 38, a carter, and William Martin, aged 32, a plumber, were charged with having wilfully murdered Hugh Knight, at Liverpool, on the 20th December. A man named James Page, a painter, was also included in the original indictment, but the grand jury threw out the bill against him. Mr. Aspinall, Q.C., and Mr. M'Connell prosecuted, and Dr. Commins defended. It appeared that on the 20th December last the two prisoners and Page were together with the deceased in the Great Eastern public-house, Langdale-street. A dispute arose amongst them, and Millichip threatened the deceased. They all went out, when the deceased, it was alleged, was violently assaulted by the two prisoners, knocked down, and kicked several times. The deceased was rescued by some women, and tried to get away, but he was followed by Millichip, who knocked him down again, his head striking the stones with great force, and he died soon afterwards.—The jury acquitted Martin, but found Millichip guilty, and he was sentenced to 20 years' penal servitude.

believe in Fate or Free will?  As another relative recently said to me.

**What do you think?**

My mum Bridget (Bridie) was my grandad Leonard and my nan Sarah Ellen O'Neill's eighth child. Ellen's parents, Michael and Mary

Ann, took the boat over from Wexford, Ireland, to Liverpool around 1875. They lost none of their traditional, dominant Irish culture on arrival, settling into the Roman Catholic ghetto that was Kirkdale and the terraced streets between Vauxhall Road and Stanley Road and passed on their culture, superstitions and love of God to the next generation.

That my grandad Leonard Gill was English and a protestant to boot was tolerated  and celebrated when he converted to Catholicism becoming rather devout it seems under my nan's influence.  The O'Neills and then the Millers, and perhaps now the Gills have a strong

matriarchal streak, the females of the species used to exerting their
influence and usually getting their way eventually. To this day Vicky
my daughter has a notice in her house; it reads "I should have done it
the way my wife told me in the first place!".

As I said earlier, Leonard Miller was a quiet, working-class man
who liked a drink; his cart horse was apparently trained to take him
home when he rolled out of the pub too drunk to drive his cart; most
men in that society did: it was women who brought up the children
and ensured that what money had been earned was spread to feed the
family.

My mother, who was one of eleven, talked fondly of her childhood
which was happy and tribal. She was heartbroken by three deaths.
Her brother Len, after whom I am named was killed a few days after
D-Day in Normandy blown up by a landmine and buried still in
France. Her father Leonard who died within a year of her marriage
from lung cancer though she always thought that catching pneumonia
at her January wedding in the snow carried him off. And her youngest

and closest brother Jimmy. A
giant of a man who had been a
merchant seaman during the
war and had five children
before his death from lung
cancer at the tragically young
age of 38.

I do know that she and my
father had very different
upbringings. The tragedy of
Dad's childhood was that his
younger sister Joyce had died

24

from meningitis when she was around four. It's more than possible that this sadness stopped both parents from wanting to repeat the large families that they had been part of. Or maybe it meant my Protestant grandparents had more freedom of choice than the generations before them, a situation anathema to traditional Catholic

communities.  For sure, it was nothing that either set of grandparents broached with anyone but themselves.

Probably the most amazing discovery is that my mother's great-grandfather and my father's great-grandfather were . . . brothers. Both Millers from the countryside north west of Lancaster near Ingleton. Nanny Gills mother was thus a cousin of mums father though I doubt if either party knew.

The saying that the past is a different country refers to different attitudes not locations. Geographically, families lived for centuries within the same relatively small area.  It was only with the industrialisation of the nineteenth century that populations moved to the cities and regarded themselves in my family's case as Liverpudlians.

Actually I have traced my family right, right back, and the highest probability is that most of the branches were Scandinavian in origin, or the last vestiges of the dark age Romano-British populations.

In researching the past though there is aways more to discover. The more you discover the more fascinating it becomes.  A past of a million stories.

# Diaspora

## 'They've all passed on, God rest 'em, but left me caught between,
## That awful colour problem of the Orange and the Green.'

('The Orange and the Green' - The Irish Rovers, 1967)

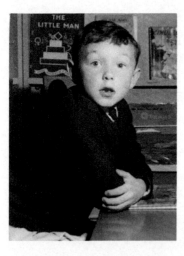

One of life's certainties is that when someone tells you, *'Keep doing that, and you'll fall'* – fall down you do.

I found this out at age three and a half at the chip shop below our one-bedroom council flat in Kirkby, near Liverpool. It was Maundy Thursday, and Mum had taken me downstairs to buy fish for our tea the next day, Good Friday, when all the shops were shut and eating meat was prohibited by the church. I was keen on Clint Walker (Cheyenne Bodie the cowboy) and cowboy films in general. I used to skip along pretending to be riding the range or charging, U.S. cavalry style, into battle. Whilst Mum joined the queue, I skipped about, a small, happy boy riding his imaginary horse on the tiled floor of the chip shop.

'Stop it, Leonard,' said Mum. 'You'll fall if you don't –' she cautioned, just as I slipped on a dropped chip and fell headlong through the plate glass window of the chip shop.

My face took the full brunt. Within moments, there was more blood than ketchup in the place and my left cheek was literally hanging off and my nose split in two. Mum whisked off her headscarf to better hold my face together as we waited for the ambulance to

arrive. I remember humming Cheyenne's theme tune to calm myself as we blue-lighted it to Alder Hey Children's Hospital. I was encouraged to sing the tune quietly by the nurse and doctor to distract me later when they stitched my face under local anaesthetic. Whilst it must have taken painful weeks or months to heal, I don't recall feeling overly self-conscious about the resultant scar, which I have to this day: except when I reached teen-age and began looking for girls to date! Years later, when I had little children of my own, I'd joke how I was an alien who had been born with three ears. The scar was from where the third ear had been removed!

Did this dramatic accident go on to make my mother overprotective of me? Perhaps. But she had other reasons to be so too.

I was born on 16th December 1956 in Walton Hospital, north Liverpool, and lived initially with my mum and dad at Dad's parents' house in Etna Street where he and his sister Joyce had been born. The terrace house had been built in the early 1800s and had originally been a rural two up and two down workers cottage. Nan and Grandad, both from the immediate vicinity married in 1926 and

moved into number 8. Nan worked in the Rea Metal widow factory just yards away from their house and Grandad was based in the bus shed which again was less than 100 yards away. The house – which had an outside loo and a backyard – was about the size of my garden log cabin today!

At 32 (Mum) and 30 (Dad), my parents were then considered old to become first-time parents. Most people at that time married and started a family in their early twenties. It's curious that one of my first memories is of the day that Mum went on the bus to hospital to give birth to my brother Ian. I can see her now walking from our street onto the main road, Green Lane, where buses trundled past; I waved and cried and was gathered up and taken back inside by my nan who assured me that she would be back soon and distracted me with a union jack flag and a sweet. I say 'curious' that I should remember this day in April 1959 because so much of my childhood altered and was held in check by the arrival of my brother.

Ian is severely disabled and today, aged 63, enjoys a protected yet limited life in a residential care home. When he was born, doctors swiftly recognised that he was a 'rhesus baby' – whereby the different blood groups of mother and baby mean that an immediate blood transfusion within hours of birth is often necessary for the newborn to survive. That is not a problem today due to medical advances, but it was dramatic in the 1950s. I don't know how well this and other early treatment was handled, but the result was that Ian was afflicted with cerebral palsy (spasticity as it was called then); he would never develop speech; he would be deaf (although not profoundly) and would need a pushchair and nappies until he was ten.

31

The effect on everyone in the family was immense. At first, it would have simply been recovering from the shock of Ian's dramatic birth. It wasn't until my brother was nearing two and failing to mirror her other grandchildren's developmental milestones of crawling, walking and talking that Nanny Miller who was the family matriarch began to say, *There's something wrong with that child.'* As a woman who'd had eleven of her own, she would not be silenced. Reluctantly and slowly, years of hospital and developmental assessment appointments began.

My father had a job as a gearbox fitter and was a regular working man. Each evening when his shift at the Ford factory finished, and he wasn't on nights (he did two weeks of days and two weeks of night in

rotation) he'd go for a couple of pints with mates. A quiet man, my surmise is that he kept his feelings about Ian to himself. Whilst the family watched TV in the living room, he'd sit alone in the kitchen, often listening to classical music on the transistor radio and rolling his own from his ever present tin of Golden Virginia tobacco and cigarette papers on an arcane machine that it seemed at the time that every man had. His first cigarette was smoked moments after he rose

from bed, usually not long after dawn.  His last he smoked in bed after
he put out the light.

His role in bringing up his children seemed to be keeping my
mother calm so that she could cope, rather than anything active of his
own. I see now the care he took to never say the wrong thing, to
smooth over cracks. My mother took antidepressants called "purple
hearts" then, following a severe nervous breakdown when I was about
four and Ian about two, and the severity of his handicap had become
obvious.  Dad trod as carefully around her as you'd avoid eggshells on
a carpet floor. There would be no more children.

Thankfully, Ian was rarely violent. When he was three, he lashed
out at me with the fire poker to split open my head but I suspect I was

to blame for whatever reason. But I can't remember anything else.
Rather, there was my own held-in anger to him. For a young boy
wanting to be out with lads his own age, I was handicapped by Ian. I

felt embarrassed that, wherever I went, Ian had to come along too. *'Take Ian out with you,'* Mum would say, and I'd worry lest the kids I played in the street with would laugh at a seven-year-old wedged in a pram. Other times it would be *'Mind Ian for me, will you, whilst I pop to the shops.'*

I kept my feelings of frustration to myself. Even as a very young boy, I was aware I was luckier in life than my brother. Only once did I give in. I was eight when Ian and I were playing in the grass. The day was so hot that I was in shorts, Ian in nappies. I could see the red ants' nest, and I didn't move him away when he went to sit on it. *'Why's Ian screaming?'* Mum yelled out from the house. *'No idea,'* I lied.

Deafness was Ian's first diagnosis because that was the easiest. For a while, he attended the Liverpool deaf school for assessment after assessment; but his movement and cognitive difficulties were profound. Mum hated it when he was sent to a residential school in Hertfordshire run by the Spastics Society now known as Scope, after a series of short stays in Victorian era assessment centres which were horrific. *'He's not going anywhere again,'* said Mum, so he simply came home and stayed with her, in her care, until he was in his late 40s, and she was too frail.

A double bed, a small single and a cot were all squeezed into the single bedroom of our family's first flat. Kirkby Newtown – to give it its full title – was the model for a popular TV police series of the day. Z-Cars (named for the Ford Zodiac cars the drove) which abbreviated our area to Newtown in the series. But the high drama and violence faced by the police were the same on screen as happened around me.

One night, Dad got involved. *This is happening too often* he told Mum as they looked out the flat window to yet another fight kicking off below on the street. He pulled on trousers, a shirt and shoes and went straight to the fight. *'Be careful Teddy',* said my mum, *'don't worry'* he said, *'I'll be fine'.* Four 'Teddy' boys were giving each other what for – Dad waded in and laid them out. Then he noticed a Lancashire police officer standing in the shadows.

*'Why didn't you stop the fight?'* asked Dad. *'You seemed to be coping well, so I just left you to it,'* came back the surprising reply!

My dad was a quiet and unassuming man, I never saw him be aggressive with anyone but he told me years later that he had learned to handle himself in the army and was surprisingly skilled at the dark arts of unarmed combat. He walked the rougher parts of Huyton and later Cantril Farm with impunity and always carried a rolled up Daily Mirror which he showed me could be bent to create a remarkably effective semi lethal weapon.

We moved from the flat when I was around four. So, other than that fight and the chip shop incident, my memories are snatches. They include watching Gerry Anderson's TV puppet show Four Feather Falls, the health visitor calling to give Mum an iron injection and my sitting on a drawing pin (and the two of us both having pain in the same place, same time!).

I can also remember watching Popeye on the black and white TV and then asking Mum to buy me spinach – and her returning with spaghetti hoops, insisting that the 's' on the can meant the rest of the word was spinach. I couldn't yet read, but I wasn't fooled.

The move from Kirkby was prompted by a neighbour dispute. That neighbour was prosecuted over something to do with my mother's job at the laundry, I think, and the council rehoused us to a prefab at Huyton, some six or so miles from central Liverpool.

# She stole neighbour's postal draft

Florence Annie Astall (aged 27), Broad Lane, Southdene, was conditionally discharged for 12 months at Liverpool County Magistrates' Court on Friday, for stealing a postal draft valued 6d. and for obtaining £12 10s. by means of a forged postal draft.

Astall, also pleaded guilty to both summonses, was ordered to pay £2 3s. costs.

Insp. H. Yates, prosecuting, said that on 23rd January, a postal draft for £12 10s. was posted to a Mrs. Gill, 3a, Broad Lane, as a maternity grant. Mrs. Gill did not receive it.

## DENIED IT

On 26th January, the draft was cashed at Broad Lane Post Office, Southdene, and the £12 10s. was paid to the person cashing it. The draft bore the signature "B. Gill."

On 9th June at Kirkby Police Station, Mrs. Astall was seen by Det. Con. McCombe, but she denied all knowledge of the matter. Later the same day, she returned to the police station and said: "I have come to tell you the truth. I stole the postal draft and cashed it at Broad Lane Post Office." She then made a statement of admission.

In court, Astall apologised for the offence, saying she did not know what made her do it.

Our prefab had been set down in 1946 to rehouse people whose original homes had been destroyed during the Blitz. There were 72 prefabs in our square and, at most, four cars.

I enjoyed playing in our large garden or out in the Close, so much that I didn't want to go to St Columbus Catholic Primary School on my first day, nor on the second. But I adapted, as kids do, and I did fine enough – I was in the high achievers' A-stream, always within the top four of my class.

There was no pressure from home to excel. When I

39

asked to join the library, Mum refused – because she said the books wouldn't be clean if someone else had read them before! I did read, though, because mum and dad bought me Swiss Family Robinson and Treasure Island at Christmas one year. At school, I followed the rules, especially concerning giving the Protestant primary school a wide birth. Go within 600 yards, and you could expect to be set upon. Always gangs of lads would hang around, hoping for trouble. I don't think anyone our age cared about which religion kids were. It was contrived, just like the greaser versus skinhead fights that older teenagers would get sucked into.

All my wider family lived in council houses, few people owned their houses; no one had a professional job. Yet for the 1960s, we weren't very poor though mum bought most things on credit even then. I knew that because of my cousin Winnie and her family.

Winnie was my Nan's older sister Etta's daughter and about ten years younger than nan. Winnie lived in a slum house about a hundred yards from nan's in Etna Street the other side of Green Lane near the Borax factory. The family consisted of Winnie who was middle aged and her husband Jack. They couldn't have children but had adopted three orphans, the oldest one was about twelve at the time, I was about four but my memories of their house and street are vivid. They had so little money that she fed Jack on cat food. Jack was too sick to work, probably with TB or some other wasting disease. He was stick thin, as thin I remember as the photos we saw of the concentration camp victims in Belsen. He was clearly too ill to work though she worked as a launderers with nan. Winnie's son Donald did have a job, slaughtering chickens at the abattoir next door even though he was only twelve. He did this ghastly trick with chicken feet

    he brought home, pulling the tendons with his hands and making
them appear to be alive.

**It terrified me**

41

At that time, all houses smelled of the soot of the coal fires and the heavy smoking of those who lived there. Very likely all this covered up the stench of decay, dirt and sickness that greased the walls of Winnie's house. When people today say they struggle with mortgages or utility bills – it bears no comparison to how unremittingly bleak life was in 1960s Liverpool for people like Winnie and her family.

Our family always worked hard. My parents did, and Nan and Grandad on Dad's side both had jobs. Grandad switched from driving trams to driving buses, and Nan, worked at a laundry which had been owned at one time by her own mother Mrs Millikin. It was because of nan that mum got the job at the shop in Kirkby and the flat with it. The Derwent laundry employed mum, nan, two of nan's sisters and

Winnie. It had after all been nan's mum's own family business once before the old lady died. Sometimes, she'd take me with her: I'd sit and play with small toy horses whilst she worked. When I went back to

her home, if I could, I'd snuggle with their English bull terrier Peggy in the dog's basket!

I spent most of my time in nan's in those early years I played in the street which was free of traffic and very narrow, we knew everyone in the road, they had all lived there since the 1930s. I would go with nan to the local shops in Old Swan, especially Shaw's butchers who made the nicest sausages I have ever tasted to his own secret recipe. When he died he took his recipe with him. Even his wife's sausages were never quite the same. Every day we got milk from the cow keepers because you could be sure the milk was 'TT' (tuberculosis tested) These urban mini dairies were on every sixth or so street and the one we used was next door to the Bus Shed . A single cow or two lived in someone's backyard – so that its owners could sell milk to their neighbourhood.

Mr and Mrs Gill holidayed in Torquay and the Isle of Man – status trips in those days. They loved to spoil their only 'regular' grandchild poor Ian was a rare visitor and was a constant source of friction and hostility between my mum and my grandad who took no prisoners when it came to disability. Metal horses. Go-carts. Torchy the Battery Boy hats. Airfix models – at one point, some thirty planes dangled from my ceiling. They also gave me four shillings and sixpence weekly pocket money, which I spent on chewing gum and, later, on collecting cards: 'The Beatles'; the American Civil War; and later Horses of the World Cards.

I say 'regular' grandchild not to be harsh on Ian, but with reference to how disabled people were treated a generation ago. Television programmes like Call the Midwife, which is set in the 1960s and features a character who has Down's Syndrome, don't tell it like it was. Society was cruel to children like my brother. Often, it was Dad and I who would visit my grandparents whilst Mum and Ian stayed home or went to visit her own mum in 'Town'.

My parents had a mixed-faith marriage. They'd met when my mother's work friend introduced them. Madge, who worked alongside Mum in a tin factory, was dating Dad's cousin George, and a double date had been arranged. The difference of religion didn't matter: Dad converted from Protestant to Catholic on marrying, and there'd always been the usual understanding that any children would be brought up Catholic.

But the chasm between the two families was as obvious as the colours orange and green. When Protestant Ulster politician Ian Paisley came on TV, Mum would throw her slippers at the television!

Mr and Mrs Gill were flag-waving Unionists who loved all things royal. Hundreds of linen Union Jack flags and banners were brought down from her attic stored there since VE Day to celebrate important dates – the coronation, Princess Margaret's wedding. Handily for me, those flags made excellent props for dressing up as a knight. When one tore or blew away, I ran home and it was almost instantly replaced.

Grandad retained his deep suspicion of Catholics. When I was around seven and working as an altar boy, it was sometimes my duty to check and then lock the church of an evening before depositing the key at the priest's house. One September night, it was dark and spooky, yet Grandad would not come inside to help, for fear or distaste.

*'God will strike me dead if I go inside,'* he told me. Family history always had it that, so strong was his view, he didn't attend his own son's wedding. Whilst putting everything together for this book, I found a photo that partially disproves that:

Whereas Nan and Grandad Gill liked roasts on Sunday – lamb one week, chicken the next, quiet fireside evenings with Embassy cigarettes for her and Players Navy Cut for him – the Catholic side of my family knew how to celebrate. At New Year, we'd head for the republican area of Litherland in the north of the city, where my mum's sister Aunty Mary lived, and there would be dancing in the

streets as people piled in and out of each other's houses. These
adults, who were my aunts and uncles and their neighbours, would
sing Irish rebel songs and drink – and there would be open cash
collections for the IRA.

For all my closeness to my nan and grandad Gill which remained until they died, I lived in a very Catholic milieu. Aunty Mary's three children, Irene, Marie and Christine were the nearest thing I had to sisters and I remained closer to them than to any of the rest of mum's large and closely knit family until I became an adult.

My maternal grandfather, Leonard Miller born in 887; died in October 1955, just months after Mum's wedding in the January of that year. My Nan Sarah Ellen O'Neill, was born in 1886 and known as Nelly. She was a hale and hearty woman who bore eleven children who clearly took their toll on her bones. After my Grandad Miller died, the year I was born she went into hospital for a routine infection and helping another patient to the toilet, slipped and fell in the sluice and broke her hip so badly it shortened one leg by almost three inches. She was confined to a chair and walked painfully with two wooden sticks and a built up clog on one foot by the time I have memories of her. She never recovered and in her old age, with improved resources in the NHS her sticks were replaced by a wheelchair which she never lost.

She lived with her two unmarried daughters, Nellie and Theresa, in what had once been a bustling, purposeful home for a large growing family. Now that no youngsters lived in the house, the place felt aged, sterile. Grandma Miller had a way of keeping me in order, saying, *'You can go upstairs, Leonard, but you can't open that drawer or go in that room.'* If I transgressed, she'd whack me across the head so hard that the chunky gold rings on her wedding finger dug into my scalp. I came to look at her bony hands as much as her face when I visited – I was never as comfortable there as I was in the Gill's house.

When I was around seven, Mum managed to get Grandma Miller and those two harridan spinster sisters a prefab opposite to ours. Dad dug up the hedge to join our gardens but – thankfully for me– lived separate lives in our own houses though mum spent most of the day with her own mum while I was at school and I visited after school every night before tea..

My nan stayed in her Prefab for about four years. Looking back she must have been lonely and incredibly bored. Nellie and Theresa worked every day and apart from mum, a visit from Aunty Mary every fortnight or so and the occasional visit from her other children and their own children she spent the days in the prefab alone. The Close was very quiet almost rural and for a woman used to sitting on the step watching the close knit community of the inner city go by, and the bustle of such a large family it must have been hard.

Her hearing had started to go a bit and she had never learned to
read or write. Her only entertainment was the television and in those
days there was just an hour of Welsh language TV in the mid
afternoon. She couldn't even knit because she had severe arthritis in
her hands. A condition she passed to all of her daughters incidentally.
For only two weeks a year was TV available from early morning to tea
time. Wimbledon fortnight. Unfortunately this usually coincided
with good summer weather and atmospheric interference causing

'snow' visual disturbance to the TV picture and loud whistling requiring the sound to be turned down. What a life!

Both nan's prefab and ours were kept in very good order. My dad undertook repairs as necessary and the houses and gardens were spotless. Despite this the day of the prefab was drawing to an end and the whole estate was slated for demolition by early 1969. This of course co-incided with my fourth year of junior school (year 6 now) so most of it was lost on me with the fast approach of the 11+ exam and the terror of failure and exile to St Columba's secondary modern where punishment beatings from older boys were routine and rife.

We were supposed to move to the newly established Cantril Farm Estate about two miles away and still being built. Those with children got a house to be mixed in with re-housed people from both north (Catholic) and South (Protestant) communities. Others like nan were destined for a high rise.

Anyway it seems my nan, at 82 and crippled, panicked about, of all things suffering the indignity of her coffin being stood on its end to come down the lift from a high rise flat to her grave. My mum, and Nellie and Theresa insist that this is what killed her along with the slow degradation of her life from Matriarch to obsolescence. Maybe a fate which awaits us all. She decided to die and did so just a month before the move and like all her generation and Irish forebears she lay in state in the front room of her Prefab for the days before her funeral. Visited by friends and relatives and kept company until her final journey to Anfield cemetery where she remains with my Grandad.

My life in the Prefab and at St Columba's primary school was the happiest part of my childhood. It represented stability and was indeed semi rural in nature which I think gave me the yearning for life in the wide open spaces of the countryside I eventually obtained. It is a great pity that the Prefabs were lost, but for the odd example in folk museums around the country. They represented a standard of comfort in housing that was decades ahead of the slums most people endured and I dare to say would probably have outlasted the slums that the new builds in estates like Cantril Farm became within twenty years. But maybe it wasn't the buildings that mattered, it was the people who lived in them.

St Columba's on reflection was an outstanding place. Maybe it was even a "model" school if such things existed then in policy terms

52

but it provided me and hundreds like me the opportunity to break free
of the fate of previous generations and get a ticket for Grammar
School; and in many cases University; which transformed our
prospects and created the twenty first century. There were one
hundred and twenty kids in my year in St Columba's, from the

brightest to what were later dubbed Special Needs, though those judged to be "backward" were sent to Special Schools.

Of these kids there were forty five of us in the "A" Class. We all passed the 11+ and went to various Grammar Schools around the city.

That, when you think of the backgrounds, lack of parental support in many cases and poor living conditions for many of that number is no men feat. Above all this though, whether these kids went on to University (or not in my case) and chose another path,

St Columba's gave us a special gift. The enjoyment of learning. A video stil exists on Youtube of my class in St Columba's infants which was shown in the press at the time

https://www.youtube.com/watch?v=baitIAqeydI

# Seasons in the Sun

## 'Young people are so infernally convinced that they are absolutely right about everything . . .'
### (J.K. Rowling, Harry Potter and the Order of the Phoenix)

There was no history of education in my family, but I was about to change that. Whereas my father left school at fourteen, I now hold more qualifications than one person may actually need.

Yet my school future – and possibly my entire personal happiness – depended on the colour of a school blazer: maroon or purple.

In the late 1960s, there were two elite Catholic grammar schools in Liverpool. St Edwards boys sported purple blazers. St Francis Xavier's College wore a very splendid maroon or rather Claret. For my mum, that was decision made. Her favourite colour was Maroon you see. For my part, I worked hard to ensure I passed the 11+ exam because at the secondary modern I'd go to if I failed, the younger boys were regularly beaten up by the older ones and thrown in the nettles.

SFX (as the place is called to this day) was a Jesuit college for around 600 boys. The priest–teachers, who wore long cassocks and

 lived onsite in a seminary, were ruthless in their strictness. Punishment was meted out with a ferule, a two-foot whalebone strap that red-marked your hands when whacked across them. At least by the time I went you were only hit on the hand. My first introduction to the ferrule was within a month of my illustrious college career.

On the way home we passed out of a metal pass gate into a very posh cul-de-sac of private houses. In the front garden of the first house on the right was a crab apple tree. I had never actually heard of a crab apple but as I emerged from the gate some boys were helping themselves to windfalls in the garden. Like an idiot I jumped over the low wall and joined them. As I bent down they scattered and I found my ear held tightly by a large sixth former one Mr Storey, the head boy no less. I was searched and my details taken for punishment the next day. Yes a very auspicious beginning.

Some of the priests were plain nasty. I wonder now if they were suffering PTSD from what they had witnessed as service chaplains or soldiers during the Second World War. During mass, students had to kneel upright on the parquet floor. If you grew tired and leant back on your haunches, one particularly cruel priest Father Adamson would creep quietly up and kick you from behind as hard as he could like he was taking a penalty kick. It certainly stopped the tendency to slovenly worship but as to the application of Christian values, well perhaps?

Another priest, Father McMorrow who was a French and Religious teacher was also the adjutant in charge of discipline for the school. He was about six foot and slim with snow white hair and thick white eyebrows despite only being about 50 yrs old. It was rumoured that before he had joined the priesthood he had driven a tank during the war. He had a thing about boys having the right length hair. If he thought it was too long, he'd flick your hair out over your collar with his ruler or finger as you passed him in class or in the corridor. If the hair draped over, it was detention for a first offence and a haircut overnight before reporting to his office after assembly the next morning. There was no second offence. It was simply suspension.

Weekly mass on a Thursday and benediction on Fridays were compulsory of course: the atmosphere was religious, and fervent. The highlight of the school year was the annual pilgrimage to Lourdes the Catholic shrine in the Pyrenees. Competition was keen to get on the trip, yet I did not go. Fr McMorrow (Butch as we called him behind his back of course on pain of....pain!) Came in and announced the trip. I of course had quite a strong Liverpool accent but Butch was posh and English. He asked for those who wished to go on the school trip to be quick and give our names to him. In my accent Lourdes was pronounced as LOO-ARDS but he pronounced it as LORDS which of course is correct. Tragically I was not interested in going on a cricket trip and declined. More fool me eh.

Of course, Mum had secretly hoped I might become a priest – it was the dear wish of many Catholic parents at that time and of course I might then be able to devote myself to the care of Ian when she got older . But I was doing well in class and had hopes on becoming a doctor. I achieved good 'O' Levels the equivalent of GCSEs now and chose chemistry, physics and biology at A-level.

My SFX years were reasonably happy. Despite my ignorance of pilgrimage sites, Butch liked me for some reason and I had an easier time than some. I was good at Latin which was a brownie point in my favour. The school had a fine tradition in the classics and being good at Latin was a good start.

I was not soft but not one of the hard-knocks either. A middling sort content to keep my head down largely with a small group of like minded boys, Alan Bennett my best friend, Philip Danson, Gregory Duce and Me. We made sure at the start of the year we sat together. The inside wall was claimed first by the Hard-Knocks who of course were in the football team and the back row by the next tier but we managed to claim the window row which I suppose put us third in the class pecking order. We would play football together at breaks with a tennis ball and our blazers for goal posts and were rarely bothered.

SFX was a Football school in the great eternal war between Football and Rugby. St Edwards was a Rugby School, maybe in hindsight I should have gone there. I was never picked for football or cricket both sports bored me and I ended up being left to my own devices doing athletics. The PE teachers were only interested in those who excelled in the school teams.

I found to my surprise that I excelled at shot-putt, discuss and javelin. I was wiry believe it or not but had great upper body strength and large legs. Outside school I began to go to a martial arts club in Prescot, a short bus ride away from Huyton. It was good exercise but more importantly I judged that a greater awareness of self defence might see me in good stead in this age of rival gangs of toughs based on religious divides, geographical turf, interests or even fashion! I did Judo and was rather good at it. I also tried my hand at Aikido which was actually the weapon of choice of my sensei, a wizened old postman who was about 5 foot 5 inches tall and looked at east 90 years old but could put a strapping six foot idiot on his back with no apparent effort and a sinister grin. Finally I tried Kendo, that is fighting with the bamboo samurai swords to the uninitiated, but the kit was too expensive so I never pursued it.

At this time I was still an altar boy at St Columba's church and quite senior by now. I was first choice for the plum midday Sunday mass which meant a lie-in and being away by 1 pm. I was also given

first refusal on the 'earners' of this line of work. You see even being an altar boy is not free from a little profit on the side. Weddings were most lucrative. Up to ten shillings (50p now) which was two weeks pocket money remember was common for a wedding but it was at the discretion of the best man and therefore not guaranteed. Funerals were actually charged and so a guaranteed four shillings (20p) was paid and this was not discretionary. I have never been a gambler or

entrepreneur so I usually plumped for the funerals and made a fair wage from them. There are also usually more funerals than weddings.

Anyway, I digress once more. I was talking about sport I think. Another altar boy, the head altar boy in fact who was a couple of years older than I, introduced me to the Sefton Harriers outside of school. This arrangement facilitated my athletics and enabled me to take part successfully in the Liverpool school athletics championships on a couple of occasions.

When I first went to SFX, I still lived in the Prefab. We started school in the September but didn't actually move until Easter of the first year so I still hung around with my mates from Longview who had been with me in St Columba's. Paul Donohue, my best mate went to St Edwards (unfortunately he got expelled in the fourth year having become a full on skin head by then). Michael Sullivan a small wheezy lad with flaky skin also went to St Edwards. He had old parents, older than mine even and wanted to be a pilot. I don't know if he ever achieved his ambition. Alongside me in SFX was another Paul, the brightest lad in St Columba's but from a rough family. Paul mysteriously disappeared in the second year we were told by his mum he had ringworm and could never come out. We eventually stopped going around and he never did come back to school. Michael, a boy with five sisters and an open house for us all. He went off to be a monk in the second year. We all travelled to school together on the number 10 bus, my Grandad's old route and some of the drivers still remembered me so I still got free travel at weekends.

At Thirteen , I bought my first record, 'White Horses' by Jacky. It was a fitting title because I loved everything to do with horses. I'd watch horses in fields or on cowboy films and enter competitions to

64

win one of my own!  I never did, and a good job too as I had nowhere to keep it.

www.youtube.com/watch?v=jtCNbERKvMs

65

Outside of the work-hard culture of SFX, street gangs were everywhere. At Easter we moved to Cantril Farm, known as Stockbridge Village these days. It was a massive new development that had plunged into being a sink estate even before the builders had finished building the last of the 15,000 thrown-up homes. Rehousing people from inner city slums and prefabs like ours, it was an Anti-Social Behaviour nightmare. Streets on the estate were connected by underpasses, where dodgy people would lie in wait. Crime. Violence. Unemployment. My parents were among the very few with jobs.

Yet I had difficulty making friends on the new estate, I went to Grammar school with a briefcase in my hand and was out of place with the re-housed bucks from the inner city. I had not wanted to leave Longview anyway and continued to ride on my bike every night during the summer and at weekends to play with my old mates. But the past never stays the same and my mates began to drift when they went to their respective secondary schools. Paul my mate was my first point of reference but slowly over the next two years he became a skinhead, so did I up to a point. It begins with dressing the right way to avoid victimisation. Acquisition of a white wrangler jacket, White half mast jeans and monkey boots or Doc Martens. Not only do you not get picked on but people give you a wide berth. That's all I wanted but he began to enjoy the feeling I think. Longview was a skinhead area but up the road a couple of miles, where my judo club was, was the land of the "greasers", the motorbike gangs.

The next step was the music, we listened to Motown, greasers were into heavy metal. Shortly after comes the imperative to carry a weapon, I carried a metal comb with a sharpened end, Down my sock, lethal!

66

Then Paul and his new mates who met in the evening when I wasn't around began painting graffiti and going on the offensive and that's thankfully where I drew the line. I tried to reason with Paul that he was going too far but to no avail. I stopped going to Longview slowly but surely, and next I heard he got into trouble with the Police and was expelled from St Edwards. A lucky escape for me in retrospect. My guardian angel looked over me then and many times since.

During my skinhead phase, I kept my hair short but not crazily so because I knew the SFX school rules.

*Just a trim,* 'I'd say at the barbers. Then, one weekend, a stand-in barber didn't listen and – whoosh! The head clippers were right over the top of my head.

*'Gill! What have you done to your head'* Butch's disembodied voice boomed out up the main school staircase as I tried to blend into the crowd heading upwards after assembly.

*'Gill! My office'*
*'You cannot go around school like that. What are you going to do?. You'll have to wear a wig'* I looked on mute as Father McMorrow produced a battered cardboard box.

**A box of wigs!**

There was no arguing. I picked out a brown one and felt the humiliation as I walked around school for the next two days with this thick, curly mop on my head. The object of ridicule from my peers. I never got my hair cut like that again so I suppose it was an effective lesson.

Mum had wanted to move because she wanted a house that was new and not like the older alternatives in Longview where my dad wanted to stay with his friends in the Labour and Conservative clubs.

In Cantril Farm, I was conspicuous as a grammar schoolboy. But harder to avoid than thugs were the packs of dogs that roamed the estate. Almost everyone had a dog but no-one took them for a walk. The dogs would be let out in the street to do their business and come back when they were hungry. Few if any of these dogs were neutered and no-one used a vet except to put a dog down. If there was a bitch on heat in the area a pack would quickly form consisting of up to

thirty animals all trying to mount the bitch and squabbling for their turn. I loved animals, and especially dogs. We had one of our own called Patch, there he is in the centre of the picture on the previous page. The risk though of being bitten by the hungry, over excited animals was high.

During school summer holidays, we had regular family days out. My dad's favourite place was West Kirkby crossing the Mersey to the Wirral Peninsula and to the river Dee. It was quite the trek, a ferry and three buses, and always with Ian in tow. Bizarrely, despite working with cars and being trained to drive HGVs during his war service, Dad never sought to own a vehicle. So, buses it was!

Given that we didn't have many holidays as such though, most outings and longer holidays were strictly for women and kids. Incredibly, I never took a holiday with my father. Mum, Ian and I would team up with Mum's sisters and their kids for a trip to Moreton Foreshore, New Brighton or Crosby Beach. It was what most families like ours did then. Men worked or perhaps had a cosy week at home. I got on well with Dad, but we never had much in common. It was Mum that I spent more time with.

Once, we went to Butlin's Pwllheli, which was as bright and fun as TV's Hi-de-Hi!; other times, it was to caravans in north Wales that smelled of the bottled Calor gas used to light the stove and whispering, sputtering gas-lights. My cousins Christine, Irene and Marie – Aunt Mary's children – made the holidays fun times when I didn't have others to run about and play with. We spent rainy days on dirty sandy beaches taking cover in small arcades that hadn't changed it seemed since the war!

The only foreign holiday I went on was with SFX in the second year. Well I had to go somewhere having turned down the Lourdes trip and even I knew that Germany wasn't a cricket ground! It was a walking trip to the Harz mountains in Germany and I qualified as I did extra German at lunchtime. We went by train to Harwich, then the overnight ferry to Bremerhaven and another train to Hannover. I'm afraid I went a bit mad on the boat over with Alan Bennett egging me on. We found that despite our age we were served rather easily and enjoyed our litres of German Pilsner enormously in the company of a group of girls from Norfolk I recall though before long I was too drunk to see them! It wasn't a particularly rough trip but I paid for the excesses with the worst headache I had ever experienced. Taught me a lesson though.

When I had my children, I was intensely involved with them and their activities. By contrast, I can only remember one outing on my own with Dad – a trip to Goodison Park stadium to see a local Huyton boys team play football. I remember feeling pleased he was finally taking me to the stadium and then the disappointment that it wasn't to a 'real' match. When I was sixteen, he took me for my first pint in the

pub. I was no drinker then, and beer gave me a headache. It was his world, not mine but he was reaching out to me in the only way he knew.

A happy childhood? I think so. I didn't have the expectations of today, and, as an adult, I've rarely looked back to my childhood to frame who I have or have not become. It wasn't the definitive time of my life. In many ways I would have been happier staying in Longview but my time in SFX gave me the grounding and discipline I needed in the rest of my life. Other years have been more important, more rewarding.

It is hard to think of a date that has been more important in my life than one that took place when I was seventeen though.

It was February 1974, the St Valentine's Day Dance at Broughton Hall Catholic Girls School West Derby.

71

I'd been to youth club events when I first left Longview in St
Aiden's community Hall with my mates with little in the way of
success to show. SFX was of course an all boys school and I led an
almost exclusively male life so girls in any capacity were a novelty.
This was my first school dance.

We had lobbied our own priests to host a dance given that there
were a variety of boys and girls schools around to invite but were met
with flat refusals from the hierarchy who regarded girls as at best
demonic. With significant persistence we had eventually prevailed
and flushed with a chink in their armour I was part of the negotiating
team. Father Mc Morrow's final offer however dashed our hoped of
glasnost as he agreed enthusiastically to our request on the conditions
that; first school uniform would be worn (we could live with that), the
school orchestra must provide the music (disappointing) and finally
the deal breaker. No girls were allowed! We promptly gave up. It
would be another eighteen months when the Jesuits were leaving to
be replaced by a more liberal order that SFX would host its first and as
it turned out only dance which was not a great success.

Anyway, back to fair Broughton. I looked around at the packed
school hall and felt quite the wallflower. I was in the lower sixth and
was there only because of my athletic prowess, now don't get too
excited, I did athletics and the captain of our athletics team a scion of
one the more numerous professional Catholic families the Corkhills
had a sister that went to Broughton Hall and she had a few tickets
over. Broughton was next to St Edwards and at the time they
regarded it as their exclusive turf so only the more foolhardy
interlopers from SFX attended. None of my actual mates came, just
those lads who were those I associated with on the Huyton bus home,

so by definition we were at least no soft touches having survived Huyton almost to adulthood.

*'Gill!'* Summoned my colleague, one John Conboy (football team and French!, I wasn't really in his league) – because then, in our school at least we only called each other by our surnames in best Harry Potter fashion. *'I need you! I want to dance with that girl, and she's dancing with another girl. We'll have to both go over.'*

This 'other girl' had long, dark hair that stretched down below her waist. She wore a long brown and cream cardigan – and a very short dress.

Above loud music, we introduced ourselves.

*'Hi, I'm Len.'*
*'I'm Pat.'*

When my friend moved on from his red haired dance partner, this girl and I stayed dancing.

Some songs later, I had to go to catch the last bus and she it seemed had to go home with her cousin Eileen (the girl with the dark hair above)and her mate Margaret (the red haired one above).

*'Will you give me a ring?'* I asked Pat, handing over my number and taking hers down. When she hadn't rung in a few days, I called up.

Turns out that was about the first time Patricia had decided to say she was 'Pat' – which of course is what I have called my wonderful wife ever since. She'd misheard 'Len' for 'Ken' so didn't know who I was for a moment and so had not wished to embarrass herself and call me, ah fate! but with our true names sorted out, we were on our way to becoming a happy couple! Our first date was the Forum cinema in Lime Street. The Sting, with Paul Newman and Robert Redford. Never really watched the film, to be honest.

Pat was sixteen and a half to my seventeen. Within 24 hours, I hoped she was the one for me. She was far too good looking for me

but we got on well and weeks turned into months. Every week we
would meet in Lime Street off our separate buses and pool our
meagre cash, just enough to see a film and have a pizza at Pizzaland.
In those days there were at least twenty cinemas in Liverpool city
centre but unbelievably we soon ran out of things to watch reduced
eventually to a dubbed Chinese western whose name eludes me (it
was poor in the extreme) and the final nadir, Candy Striped Nurses
which we left early to escape the dirty old men watching it.

Pat lived in Anfield, north Liverpool. Her father,Jimmy ,worked
as a site agent on a building site and was only nine years younger than
my grand-dad and oddly a very similar type of man. He had been

married twice and had two boys with his first wife Louie before marrying Pat's mum also called Pat who was herself from a close knit Catholic family who lived in the centre of Liverpool, the Murphy's.

Also living with them was Jimmy's old uncle Charlie who had given up his own house in Llandudno when his wife died and was a permanent lodger. The first time I was invited round to meet the parents, Old Uncle Charlie and Auntie Louie, Jimmy's first wife were both there, probably to way me up but maybe it was a coincidence. They were introduced as "this is auntie Louie and Uncle Charlie". I was under the impression erroneously that they were married to each other and found it a bit odd I must say until it was explained some weeks later.

It was two buses over to Anfield. We saw each other several times a week – and my studying went off the cliff. Within months of our meeting, Pat decided against school altogether and despite opposition from both me and her mum she left school and got a job in the Breck Road library with a view to applying for nurse training when places became available. It did help a bit though with films and Pizzas.

I was accepted well by her mum though her dad remained understandably hostile for some time and I suspect never really liked me though the feeling was mutual. I spent an increasing amount of time at Pats. Her mum had a close family and there were frequent family parties at the house, reminiscent of the parties we had had in Litherland when I was small but without the IRA! Anfield was not a republican hotspot, Pats Grandad Mr Murphy a proud ex Royal Marine and (though left wing), very patriotic and although they were devout Catholics like mum's family and originally Irish they were vehemently opposed to the republicans and their increasingly violent profile.

Pat's dad was a boss and had a good well paid job and lots of savings so, though they lived in an unassuming terraced house they enjoyed foreign holidays every year and always had a new car on hand. In the summer Pat said she was going on holiday to Majorca and being lovesick I was upset. Out of the blue she said her dad had offered to pay for me to go and so I had my first proper foreign holiday, the Hotel Esperanza, Alcudia Majorca ; apart from the German trip with school in the second year of course. It was splendid.

Meanwhile, my university applications were in. I hedged my bets, and as well as medicine and dentistry which in hindsight was rather ambitious even if I had been doing any work, I threw in the wild card of agriculture at Leeds. My subsequent interview shattered my illusions that academics were the all knowing individuals my teachers gave us the impression they were.

**Interviewer   Why do you want to do Agriculture here at Leeds?**

| | |
|---|---|
| Me | Well I'm good at Biology and I like animals |

| | |
|---|---|
| **Interviewer** | **'Ah, I see you live on a farm.'** |
| Me | 'Yes, I suppose I do, sort of, I live in Cantril Farm.' |

### At this point I thought he was making fun of me

| | |
|---|---|
| **Interviewer** | **'Do you grow Crops or are there Animals on your Farm?' Is this man real?** |
| Me | 'No, it's full of animals,' |
| | **I said, thinking of all those roaming dogs.** |

| | |
|---|---|
| **Interviewer** | **I will give you an unconditional offer then'** |
| Me | 'Thank you!' I replied, keeping my thoughts to myself. |

### Academics! How stupid could they be?

When my results came in, the 'Pat effect' meant I didn't get the high grades for medicine, but I still turned down agriculture, even though I didn't even need to pass. Ironically for a man who would go on to work internationally, a 90-minute train ride felt too far away for comfort. I had never been out of Liverpool. What if I had gone to Leeds and never saw Pat again.

# A Policeman's Lot

# 'Oh . . .
## When Constabulary duty's to be done,
## to be done.'
### (The Pirates of Penzance – Sir William S. Gilbert)

*'Kirkby Library. Reader's Advisor. Can I help?'*

In my summer job of stacking bookshelves and helping readers, this was a line I had delivered time and again. On that day, I was on front desk duty, and I'd said it when I picked up the telephone. I was eighteen, polite and slightly bored. The voice that replied had an Irish brogue.

*'There's a bomb in your library, You've got 20 minutes.'*

The IRA. I knew who they were – as did everyone in Britain.

This was July 1974, and some months earlier, the Irish terrorists had expanded their violence to mainland UK. That February 12, people, including two children, had been killed when a bomb exploded on a bus transporting soldiers and their families in

Yorkshire. Ever since, there had been attacks and threats. Especially in major cities, you began to get used to buildings being temporarily closed or cordoned off due to a bomb threat.

I remember not being scared at all. In fact, it was exciting and a bit of a rush when a police officer arrived, took a statement from me and conducted a cursory search of the library. We'd closed the library, of course, and were directed outside. *'Give it half an hour. Then you can go back in,'* the officer said.

Which is what we did. No bomb. No drama. But for me, my future took an unexpected turn.

I could do that; I'd thought as I watched the police constable who was only a little older than me, handle the situation. All the mystique about being a policeman that had, I'd felt, put the job out of my reach had been dispelled. Could be quite an exciting job, too, I remember thinking.

The next day at work, I searched out a book: A Policeman's Lot by Peter Nobes. Published in 1973, it detailed his career. The idea was growing . . .

Less than a year later, I would be the one attending a bomb call at a small council house in Huyton.

As I entered the council house in Kipling Avenue, the family of three adults and two children were sat around a round smoked glass table transfixed by a six-inch cube covered in brown paper and sealed with tape that had arrived in the post. Their son was a soldier serving in Northern Ireland, and there was an Irish frank mark on the package.

On that day, I picked up the parcel, carried it into the garden and placed it in a bucket of water. Stupid really. When bomb disposal arrived, they told me I could have lost an arm. Or worse. No evacuation for me, just bravado. Oh the naivety and stupidity of youth!

All through my career and since people have asked me why I joined the police, I mean there was hardly a history of policing in the family apart from my grandad's brief dalliance as a wartime special and I knew no policemen myself. I do remember that my cousin Irene who babysat me as a child told me after I joined that she wanted to join the police but when she went she was too short at five feet three inches. The answer people always wanted was that I had a sense of public service, that I wanted to help people or catch criminals or make society better, and indeed I have many times given the customer the answer they wanted.

But this is a memoir, a time for truth, at least about things that matter less than they once did. The answer to why I wanted to be a policeman really was the uniform. I really am as shallow as I accused my mum of being choosing my school on the basis of a claret blazer.

Just a small delve into my thinking might be useful here. My dad was in the army in the second war as were all my uncles so the mid fifties were a time when uniforms and military service were normalised. My Grandad was a bus driver, uniforms again you see, and when they moved to Huyton they lived next to the Territorial Army (TA) barracks. I had a yearning as a small boy to join the boys brigade who marched out every Sunday from St George's C of E church near the prefab but mum wouldn't hear of it; it was too like the Orange Lodge you see. Dad wouldn't let me join the scouts because he said the scoutmasters were strange and not in a good way! By the time I went to SFX I really wanted to join the TA but it was too time intensive and I was too young.

I travelled to school on two buses, the second was the 81 along Queens Drive which stopped at Taggart Avenue Childwall two stops before SFX. On that bus a group of Police cadets got off to continue their onward journey and I envied them. I think at that point I started to mull over being a policeman.

I sort of surreptitiously took the plunge a couple of weeks after my last A level exam. I think I had decided at that point that whatever happened I was going to reject university and had already secured a job at Kirkby library, ostensibly a summer job but with the possibility of permanency if I wanted it. It was the first week of July and Pat and I went to the Liverpool Show which was as big as the county shows we have today and a major event. I visited the police recruitment stand and got the brochures and was immediately hooked.

By the autumn my application was in and I was given an interview date. I was greeted and informed that the entrance test was in the main hall. As I walked in I was drawn to one side by a Sergeant who was supervising the test. *'You don't need to sit the test, son, seeing as how you have A-levels. But we would like you to have a go so we can gauge the level'.*

So I did. It was insultingly easy. Entrance to the police in September 1975 needed fitness and common sense – but not

Chief Constable James Haughton with the longest line-up of recruits in the history of police forces on

Recruits line-up a record the police force on Merseys

academic rigour. One test consisted of scanning three pages of the telephone directory, where all the listings were 'Smith' except for the single entry for the name 'Jones' that you had to find and circle but there were a wide range of candidates, the lad next to me was scratching his head and whispered, *'God, this is hard isn't it?'* I suspect he didn't get in but the Police were severely under strength at the time so maybe he did!.

Merseyside Police was formed in 1974 to serve a population of more than a million people. On 29th December 1975, I was one of 165 cadets – the largest intake ever to attend the Merseyside Police Training Centre in Mather Avenue which was two buses from Cantril Farm. We were sworn in and then led to the large WW2 era gym hall

where five men from the stores in brown overalls sized us up in a few seconds and threw a variety of uniform items at us. If an item was too big the response was, *'You'll grow into it son.'* If it was too small, *'Well lose some weight then.'* But their judgement was on the whole pretty accurate and by the end of the day we donned our uniforms and began to look the part at least.

Training took place in Bruche Training Centre Warrington until March 1976, and I found I enjoyed being away from home, as long as I saw Pat at weekends.

The first Sunday I went by train and it seemed to take hours. I was met at Warrington station by a geriatric minibus and herded into it, then on to Bruche to be allocated a surprisingly modern and comfortable room and introduced to my Training Sergeant Ray. I was in K Class and K Block as it happens, easy to remember.

Days began with an hour's marching, then continued with classroom training and 'practical scenarios' around the centre which was laid out like noddy's village with road signs and mocked up buildings.

The initial training course lasted ten weeks, an eternity, I had never been away from home longer than the two weeks in Majorca before. I enjoyed it though and excelled managing to get the award of top student for an average of 100% across all my weekly tests, I received a prize of a set of Police Law books and wore a blue lanyard as a mark of distinction.

The course wasn't all work though and we had a couple of formal events where we had to hire evening dress and I was able to meet Pat off the train and book her into a local pub overnight (while I stayed at the centre and had to be in bed; lights out by 11pm of course!)

The lads and girls in my class were a nice bunch and drawn from Cumbria, Lancashire, Greater Manchester, Cheshire and the Isle of Man as well as Merseyside. I mated up with Steve from Cheshire who

I still see almost 50 years on, and a lad called Peter from Cumbria who I heard a few years back had a bad accident and took early retirement. We lost one girl from the class after about eight weeks when she was suddenly arrested one day for having a boyfriend who was a bank robber. It turned out she had been a Go-Go dancer before she joined in Manchester, but the Police were desperate to recruit so maybe that was the problem!

I found the domed high helmet awkward to wear. Mentally, I was also weighed down with worry over what others might think. When I stepped onto the street, it felt like everyone was looking at this young chap in a big hat. Then I realised that people were looking at me just as they might any oddity on the street. They'd glance across – then move on!

My mum and Dad and Pat attended the graduation and Pass out Parade in March of 1976 and it was a proud day. I felt on top of the world as we performed our 'continuity drill' faultlessly to the recorded strains of a marching band played over a tannoy system.

Weeks later, I could call Pat my fiancée. I never said, *'Will you marry me?'* but we had an agreement. I'd paid £80 of my £113 month's salary on a ring, and we held an engagement party at the police social club. With a few friends each from school.

I was 20 years old. Life was good. I was ready to do a job I'd been trained for and my future was dropping into place at my first posting; Huyton Police Station.

# Huyton, Huyton Two Dogs Fightin'

**'He never can stop laughing. He says he has not tried;**
**And once he did arrest a man**
**And laughed until he cried.'**

('The Laughing Policeman' – Charles Penrose)

*'Mister Gill,'* said the sergeant, *'you are on the Roby and Swanside beat.' 'Here'*, he says pointing to the map. *'This is the boundary, Page Moss Lane, this side is ours, the other side is Liverpool City.'*

*'OK Sarge I said, but what if I see something on the other side of the road?'*

*'Listen Mr Gill, the other side of the road is Liverpool. We do not Police Liverpool. If, in the unlikely event that you see a Liverpool bobby you don't speak to him or acknowledge him or you my son are for the high jump. What's more if you see the Liverpool jeep, you jump behind the nearest hedge and hide until its gone. They will be up to no good and will only get you into trouble. A belly full of ale and a boot full of loot that's all they are. Remember I'll be watching you."*

It was my first day on my own as a patrol officer at Huyton in what I thought was K Division of the Merseyside police. I could just as easily have been posted to C Division which was the other side of Page Moss Lane and presumably filling my belly with ale and loading my boot full of loot but Sergeant 52 otherwise known as the Bacup Ram in the county of Lancashire seemed to think different. He it seemed was still of the belief that we were in Lancashire Constabulary.

Sergeant 52 (Lenny), the first Lenny I had ever met not from my family, was in his early fifties but looked over 60 and had a girth like my own today, making him the image of the laughing policeman, but he didn't laugh much. He and most of the policemen at Huyton, Kirkby, Halewood and Prescot which constituted K Division were the flotsam of Lancashire Constabulary who had been stranded when Merseyside was formed almost two years earlier having been posted there as a punishment for some real or imagined misdemeanour and were condemned never to return. In Lenny's case he was a bit too fond of the ladies he claimed. He was the station Sergeant and senior to Carl, a marathon runner who was the street sergeant but it was Lenny who ruled the roost served with a fresh pint of tea on the hour who gave us our instructions. So off I went into the weak afternoon sun that late April afternoon.

In the late 1970s, policing was almost entirely about being out on your beat. On each shift, I had to walk around my beat twice; once before my break (the scoff break) and once afterwards. I'd get called to a job via my radio. But in between, I was to patrol purposefully. I'd walk 25 miles in a shift as I checked shops were secure but looked for trouble, really, because then I might be able to prevent it.

While walking was the normal means of getting to calls, it was common to flag down and 'commandeer' black taxis who gave free rides in an attempt to keep on the right side of the police. It was also quite common to flag down private cars and demand to be taken to a job. Very few people complained and rather enjoyed helping the police and pretending to be driving a police car, especially as we 'allowed' them to ignore red traffic lights in the days before health and safety and traffic cameras proliferated.

Paperwork at the station was squeezed into the final 30 minutes of each shift and woe betide you if you were caught by the street sergeant malingering in the station at any other time, otherwise you would acquire the moniker the 'Station Cat" and persecuted as a result.

Just as today, shifts were a mix of earlies (6 a.m. to 2p.m.), lates (2 p.m. to 10 p.m.) and nights (10 p.m. to 6 a.m.). Each had a flavour of its own.

Earlies were dominated by sorting out overnight car thefts and burglaries to shops, sheds and homes. I would parade on at 5.50am and be out of the station after a quick cuppa by 6.10. At that time of day there were few people about and only the early newsagents open so that would be the first target to stop for a warm and a gossip about what was happening in the area (we call it intelligence gathering these days). Three or so Newsagents premises later the school kitchens would start to open and a drop in for more gossip of a different tone and stripe accompanied by a bacon sandwich or piece of toast. At this point the first jobs would come in and life was quite busy for a couple of hours till it was time to walk in or be picked up by the covering panda car for our 'scoff' and 45 minutes uninterrupted snooker.

The second session was usually busier and punctuated only by opportunities to persecute a few motorists or wander around the backs of houses or shops looking for vulnerable spots to remember later in the day, with a stop for tea at the library maybe or butchers for a sausage butty. Butchers are surprisingly knowledgeable about what is going on.

Lates began with a 2 p.m. parade at the station, then were mainly spent on patrol. There was generally more time to think and less opportunities for tea in the afternoon as shops were busier. This was the time that having friends or relations on your beat were useful. My Auntie Emma lived on the Roby beat and I would visit her or the parents of some of my mates from school who would feed me and tell me of the progress of their offspring and let me rest my feet for a few minutes.

After scoff on afternoons though was a nightmare. Anti Social Behaviour as it is called now was just called 'complaints of youths' and domestic violence called simply 'domestics'. These would come in hard on each others' heels and I would be run ragged from 6pm until being picked up at 10pm or so to go off duty though with luck and a streak of ruthlessness an arrest could be made around 9.30pm for a couple of hours overtime processing it at time and a half. The closer

97

it got to 10pm the less mercy or discretion would be available to lippy youths or belligerent husbands!

In 1973 Elton John released a record which reached number one. It was called 'Saturday Night's Alright for Fighting' and could have been an anthem for the times. Well at Huyton any night was alright for fighting, except maybe Mondays and night shift was designed for it. We started at 10pm because the pubs let out at 11pm and from half an hour before when the landlords shouted last orders the fighting would start.

Today it seems that fighting is a nasty lethal affair, we hear of record stabbings and shootings, the murder rate is at an unprecedented level and fights are vicious short affairs with weapons used quickly and brutally. In the 1970s fights were longer drawn out affairs. Mostly, it was fist fights: really large groups would brawl in the street and then very quickly punch themselves out. there was little recourse to weapons unless it be chairs and tables and the injuries were broken bones rather than fatal penetration wounds. Fighting was more akin to a saloon brawl in a cowboy film and almost part of the entertainment. A good night out usually ended in a fight and the pubs in Huyton were, it seems, designed for it.

There were large pubs regularly spaced throughout Huyton; The Hillside, The Bluebell, The Oak Tree, TheFarmers Arms and The Eagle and Child (pictured here where it was reputed you could buy anything your heart desired) all lay along the main A57, but every beat had one or two infamous pubs in addition to these. Each one of these was a fighting pub and fights would ripple out from one to the other starting just after 10pm and lasting to 1 am. The change-over at ten meant that we could deploy the whole section to each fight in turn and put the metaphorical fires out before the next began in earnest.

I got punched a few times, but unlike now, the chances of getting stabbed were low. Crowds that were fighting amongst each other held a substantial degree of respect for the police and knew that if they crossed us we would identify them and mete out suitable justice in short order. When I had to control a fighting man, I remembered my judo skills. I'd bring the person I was arresting to the ground and then get on top of them.

My shift, two scale we were called (one of four shifts at Huyton) comprised seventeen Constables, ten 'foot patrols' each allocated to a beat, four 'panda cars' and a van each vehicle covering two foot beats. This included two Policewomen. Bernice was a very tall thin girl who looked like a blonde version of Olive Oil the cartoon Popeye's girlfriend. She was engaged to one of the more experienced bobbies on the shift and Betty a stout girl from St Helens who was as hard or harder than any of the rest of us on the shift. In addition the Prescot section which was our reserve and shared resources with us consisted of five men and two Policewomen. In 1976, 80 per cent of the foot patrols at Huyton were under twenty one.

As you see there were many more male than female officers – but one night, the reverse appeared true. Betty was posted to Huyton Village, the beat next to mine and we usually walked out and around together on nights for protection and company. As it happened I had left her in the village and walked to my own beat when I heard a call for a large fight at the Rose and Crown pub in the Village. I flagged down a taxi and hurried back arriving first and could hear chairs and glasses being smashed inside, moments later Betty arrived breathless and together we opened the side door to the bar to be met with a scene of active carnage.

I closed the door gently and we retired to the shadows and called for more help. Minutes later we heard the screaming of an engine (no klaxons then) as the Prescot car arrived screeching to a halt in the car park and out tumbled Elaine and Jean who constituted Prescot section that night. I suggested we hang on. Moments later Bernice arrived in her mini and jumped out. There were now 5 of us and not enough shadow to hide us all, it was time to go in!

Between them Betty and Elaine who could both handle themselves waded in and I managed to separate a couple of blokes and start ushering them toward the door with the help of the landlord and his bar staff. Ten minutes later we had everyone out on the car park and they began to drift away with some encouragement.

As we began to congratulate ourselves on a job well done a noisy scuffle broke out near the pub door and an enormous Irishman began laying about him. He would not be reasoned with and was continuing to fight even with the girls hanging off him.

*'If you don't go home now, I am going to have to lock you up,'* I told him.

*'I'd like to see you try,'* he growled back.

Surprisingly, we were not issued handcuffs in those days. I had found an old pair one day in the station which dated from the 1930s I think and kept them as my own pair, I still have them today, and I got them out. Popped one cuff onto my wrist – and snapped the other onto his.

*'You,'* I said clearly, *'are under arrest. I have no key for these, so if you want to get away from me, we will have to go to the police station together first.'*

*'Not likely,'* he said – or possibly something ruder. Then he strode off down the road and, because he was way stronger than me, I had to hang off him as he went along dragging Elaine and Jean too while the other two girls encouraged the rest of the revellers home.

It was scary being dragged along for 300 yards or so before the dog handler Tom and a bloody big Alsatian brought the incident to a close. The suspect and I went into the back of the dog van watched over by the snarling Alsatian. At the station, I released myself from my unlikely charge and processed his arrest. He wasn't actually a bad bloke the next day once he had sobered up. Another exciting day on the job!

There was another notable incident associated with pub fight management, this time at a call to the Bluebell pub which was incidentally the pub where my grandad drank). The Bluebell was a Bent's Brewery pub which was synonymous with fighting, maybe it was something in their beer! One night a call came in and a lad called

Billy attended and piled out of his police car, truncheon in hand to calm things down confident that his back up was on the way and would soon be with him.

I arrived in a taxi about 5 minutes later along with two other police cars and a couple of foot men but there was no sign of Billy or his car. In fact we found him safe and well in the pub with things well under control but someone had actually stolen his car when he had made the mistake of leaving the keys inside in his haste. It was found some hours later burnt out about a mile away.

On nights around 1.30 am, once the drunks finally began to go to bed we would make our way back to the station for scoff but there was also an unmanned substation we could use in Page Moss which had originally been adjacent to the Tram, later bus Terminus. One night I had been placed on one of the Page Moss beats and met up with Bob who eventually became best man at my wedding and who was on the adjacent beat.

We ate our sandwiches, made a cup of tea and put our feet up. Before we resumed, Bob asked me to fill in the visit book to say we had been there while he went to the toilet. Moments later I heard a piercing scream and Bob stumbled out of the toilet with his trousers round his ankles. I ran over to him with some concern but he began to calm down. It seemed that the light bulb in the toilet was broken so he had closed the door and sat on the toilet in the dark. Moments later he felt a sharp pain in his buttock and sprang up only to see in the gloom a huge wet rat in the toilet bowl having bitten his bottom and he had run out screaming. When I finished laughing I vowed always to check the toilet before I went and never use it in the dark.

The time from 3 a.m. to 6 a.m. was my favourite time. No matter the weather I'd walk deserted, peaceful streets and breathe in the calm. I felt the I owned the streets and shared it only with small urban animals and surreptitious criminals. If a window were to smash – I'd hear it a mile away. Typically, little happened. Perhaps the only drawback to this time of the night is the weariness which can come upon you rapidly and sometimes without warning brought on by the quiet and lack of human contact.

One night in the late March of 1977, in my second year on the beat I was the beat officer for Huyton Quarry. This covered a large council estate, like Cantril Farm but built In the early 1960s, an industrial estate and an extensive semi rural area of housing dating back to the nineteenth century. The end of my beat was marked by a bridge where the road passed over a railway line, and in the centre of that bridge was a bench.

The night was cold but dry and clear and I was suddenly bone weary. It was about 4.30am and there was not a soul or sound to be heard but for the faint screaming of a fox in the far distance. I sat on the bench for a moment in the darkness to catch my breath and enjoy the moment. I took off my helmet and placed it next to me and took a deep breath. The next I knew I was woken by the chink and whirr of a milk float. I emerged into the cold light of the morning, it was 6.15 am and I had slept soundly for almost 2 hours. It only happened the once, and I was mortified! It could have been worse and a passing wag may have stolen my helmet or worse. I ran full tilt the mile and a half back to the station but fortunately no one had missed me.

Another embarrassing moment occurred when, in an uncharacteristic outbreak of laziness (Ha!) I decided to take a short cut through a park and cut off a half mile or so on my way back to the station. In attempting to climb over the six foot metal railings my trouser leg caught on the top and I plunged into an undignified heap onto the floor and ripped my trousers. Fortunately I hit the grass and not the pavement on this occasion. It was the last time I was so careless.

At some point on every shift the 'panda driver' covering us would give us a lift for half an hour for a warm or a chat and often we might join him at one of his 'brew specs'. This was the name for all the kindly cuppas doled out to us from shopkeepers, care home staff and friendly folk. Like my Newsagents, school kitchens and butchers on earlies or my aunties on afternoons. I know of at least three marriages that started at brew specs.

Everything useful went into my pocketbook, ready to be used in evidence at court. The patrol sergeant caught up with me at least once in a shift to check on my safety and sign that my book was up to date. Every incident I attended and every summons or arrest had to be written up at the time, contemporaneously is the technical term and it was important to keep up to date and easy to get behind and spend hours of your own time at home catching up before the next visit or 'peg' as we called it. Failure to do this fastidiously would result in disciplinary action.

I had a target of 20 arrests and 30 summonses a month. That included transgressions as trivial as having no water in the washer bottle or dropping litter or as serious as dangerous driving or burglary. A high proportion of summonses though were for having an expired tax disc – which was indeed my first 'success'.

Most of us were not long out of school and looking back we must have been a nightmare to supervise. Our sergeants forced us to grow up quickly and it is a testament to their hard work and professionalism that so few of us fell by the wayside. But as we were essentially a bunch of overgrown kids practical jokes used to be very much a way of life.

Some were relatively harmless. Most new starters were given a cycling proficiency test. Such a test was entirely fictitious but the new lads and girls were required to done their full uniform including gabardine overcoat, tunic, helmet and gloves (usually on the hottest day of the year and navigate an obstacle course in the Police Station yard. After navigating emergency stops and drawing their truncheons whilst on the move whilst being clapped and heckled by the rest of the section, candidates 'graduated' to the advanced manoeuvre 'wet weather test' where the testers threw buckets of water over them as they cycled past.

At the time there were many many stray dogs handed in, some were genuine strays but many more dogs were handed in when their owners could no longer afford to keep them or get medical treatment for them if they were sick or injured. The dogs were kept in a kennel at the back of the station where they were collected by the RSPCA on a weekly basis. There were usually as many as twenty dogs the night before the collection day. A few particularly naive individuals were told to take the dogs for a walk after scoff on the night shift. Those few passers by were astonished to see an officer in full bib and tucker wearing his helmet struggling to control twenty dogs of all sizes and shapes and held in check with lengths of string. The practice stopped abruptly when one particular officer was seen by the night Superintendent who was coming to inspect the station and when challenged told him it was his nightly routine. The senior officer was not impressed.

Other practical jokes got out of hand though. My mate Bob was a very fast sprinter and could catch most things over 200 yards. To test out a probationer's courage, he'd hide in a doorway at 4 a.m. and then smash a piece of a glass just as the starter was coming along. The test was whether the chap would run away, ignore it or chase Bob. One night, the new probationer did chase Bob – what we didn't know was that he was an England sprinter and while we watched first with hilarity, then excitement and finally with horror he caught Bob in short order, truncheon in hand and battered seven bells out of him before the rest of us watching could get to him.

Another prank spooked me though because on this occasion the joke was on me. I was on the Huyton Quarry beat again patrolling the St John's estate. At this time there was a recently released organised criminal about who had vowed to murder a policeman on his release.

At 11.30pm I was sent to a report of a break in at the small library in the block of shops near the chip shop which was beginning to wind down. I'd dealt with some trouble at the chippy earlier on but found that indeed the library door had been smashed and an entry forced. As I sat inside the darkened library watching the chippy crowd disperse and the block of shops become quiet, the phone rang. What do you do? Ignore it, answer it, but it rang and rang so I picked up the receiver and said nothing.

A male voice said,

*'I'm watching you, you're alone there and I'm coming to kill you.*'

I was chilled, my mind went blank. I knew I couldn't call for assistance on the basis of a phone call so I sat there, worried and unsure what to do. Eventually, when the phone didn't ring again, I secured the door and left. I was shaking by this time totally unnerved waiting to be attacked by some unseen menace but nothing happened and I returned to the Station in one piece for scoff.

As I sat watching the snooker match the patrol Sergeant joined us and said loudly,

*I believe there was a break in Manor Farm Road tonight.*

*Yes Sarge*

*Anything unusual happen then?*

I hesitated and the whole room burst out laughing at my discomfort, but it seemed I had passed some sort of test. It turned out to be the sergeant who had made the call as a wind-up. I could see the joke at the end of the day? It had been hard to see the funny side at the time though.

But it wasn't just wind ups we engaged in which showed our immaturity. We regularly tried to see how many people we could get in a mini panda car. We got nowhere near the Guinness book of records but we did get ten people in one night before, car full, the driver did wheelies in an iced-over deserted car park.

One final memory in this vein occurred on Christmas Day. This holiday period is usually quiet and, as everybody is paid double time we worked with a skeleton staff with just two cars and six foot patrols. The Inspector and both Sergeants paraded us on and promptly went home for Christmas dinner and I volunteered to staff the station, so was given their home telephone numbers (no mobiles then!). So I sat in the station on my own with a packed lunch of turkey sandwiches. I had the switchboard to answer and a 999 phone for emergency calls, plus I controlled the radio and would answer any visitors at the desk, though it was unlikely.

I settled down to watch the Christmas film on a small portable TV and was halfway through the film when all hell broke loose. The 999 phone rang;

*Someone has stolen a Police car, it's weaving in and out of the Street lamps.*

*Oh..... OK Thanks for ringing.'*

Immediately I called the cars in turn, while answering several calls all reporting a stolen Police car.

*'Oh shit, its' us,'* came the wary reply quickly cut off amid giggling though it was impossible to tell which car was responding though I had my own suspicions.

By 8pm it was deadly quiet and the patrols appeared to have gone off the grid so I decided stupidly to lock up the station and check all the shops myself on my motorbike. It was an idiotic thing to do. Not insured, no back up, I put my safety and career in danger and didn't realise. I thought I did it for the best. But once again my guardian angel intervened, all was well and I handed over at 10pm confident in the knowledge all was well despite the best efforts of my wayward colleagues.

But all was not practical jokes, pranks and parties. We did a good job and kept the lid on an area which had one of the highest crime rates and volatile populations in the UK. Every day was an adventure and whilst I emerged without serious injury many of my colleagues didn't. We were subjected to attacks and ambushes on a regular basis and I made almost two hundred arrests in a single year largely for disorder and assault offences.

I grew up fast in those first two years at Huyton. We weren't just law enforcers, but social workers, dealing with people who had serious mental heath issues some damaged with PTSD from WW2 others living in unbelievable poverty or subject to chronic abuse from relatives neighbours or criminals. We were also the back up for just about every emergency major or minor unlike today we never refused any call for help. I would help people get into their homes when they

locked themselves out, take in stray dogs, search for missing people, help the elderly cross the road and even give the vulnerable elderly lifts to do their shopping. I knew almost everybody on my beat and they knew me by name. Many hated me but more I think saw me as a friend.

It was not just the living we dealt with but the dead too. Seeing dead bodies is something all police officers get used to. Sudden, unexplained death at a private home is not uncommon, nor is forcing entry into a property when neighbours and family can't make contact with the person who lives inside. I can still see the carpet turned red by an elderly woman whose veins had burst in her ulcerated legs, and she bled out alone and unable to move. As a police officer, you press on. You don't let your emotions derail you.

Other memories are of the shock and emotional brekdown of relatives when you tell them that they have lost a loved one. Breaking the news. Never good. In October 1976, 72A Alamein Road is called

111

out on the police radio. Neighbours raising the alarm that the elderly occupant hasn't been seen. Possible sudden death.

**My grandparents' address.**

Nan was in hospital, and I knew Grandad was on his own at home. I was the second one there, racing to the scene with dread. When I arrived the bobby who attended, an old county man fortunately met me and when I blurted out my connection with the address he refused to let me in, called the Sergeant and sent me home. My dad identified the body. I soon learnt that it was my grandad who had been discovered. He'd had an aneurism and died in his sleep. A good way to go people say, I hope so.

# We've Only Just Begun

**'Sharing horizons that are new to us**
**Watching the signs along the way**
**Talkin' it over, just the two of us**
**Workin' together day to day.'**
(The Carpenters –1970)

Forget 999 – for Pat, it's 777 that counts.

*'Why don't we get married on 7th July 1977?'* she suggested, *'Its a lucky number'*

Like all Catholics, we give great importance to superstition. I grew up with a mother who wouldn't straighten pictures and a grandmother who'd be horrified if you put shoes on the table, both signs of an imminent death in the family. A wedding that was all the sevens sounded good.

Only trouble was I wouldn't finish my probation and be confirmed as a police officer until 29th December 1977.

*'I can't risk it,'* I said. *'What if I am not confirmed and find myself with no job?'*

Because we largely thought the same, Pat agreed to marry after I had finished my probation period. While we waited, we took three good holidays. Our first outing was a package tour to Greece in the summer of 1976. As you may know the summer of 1976 was the hottest and sunniest in living memory in England so what did we do? Well we went on a Mediterranean holiday!!

It started bad and got worse but in the end we enjoyed ourselves. Our flight out was a new experience though airports even then were a fraught affair. We arrived in Athens airport en route to our resort in Rafina about twenty miles away and looked for our hotel transport. No Transport. No holiday rep. I made increasingly bemused enquiries and eventually found a rep from another (larger) company who told us our company had gone bust. This of course was before ABTA guarantees. So what next.

I decided to press on and convinced Pat, suitcases in hand to get the bus. What I didn't realise was that the Greeks still had a foreign alphabet, it wasn't just the ancients then! My limited classical education courtesy of SFX came to my aid. We made it to the bus station. I sounded out the letters of the various destinations Ραφήνα R-A-F-I-N-A. More in hope than expectation we boarded the bus, I pointed to the destination board and showed the driver our hotel name, he wrote an amount down , I paid, we drove away amid people with chickens in cages and the usual stereotypical third world public transport atmosphere.

Eventually my driver shouted something I couldn't understand and a group of kindly locals threw us off the bus at our hotel and helpfully threw our cases off too. At the reception I identified myself and presented our booking form.

Miraculously mein host in halting English told us, with the help of a passing South African guest that our room was paid for with no extras because the company had failed to pay for anything else. Well it was better than nothing. We had a room; some youthful initiative. And a pocketful of travellers cheques (no credit cards then so you bought pre-paid cheques in the denomination of that country).

The passing South African and her husband inextricably took us under their wing and took us out in their hire car for a couple of days while we acclimatised and I found out more about the local bus system. In the end it was a lovely holiday, we got about on buses, ferries and more buses. After a week I could even read Greek without sounding the letters out loud.

We were actually very fortunate on that holiday. It could have been much worse and much more costly. The firm had paid both the hotel for the room and the airline so the return flights were honoured but because I had had to organise things myself I vowed that next time I would forego a package holiday and arrange it myself.

In May 1977 we went to Italy on a grand tour. I spent the princely sum of £17.61p for an under 21 ticket for two on the Italian railways. This enabled us to travel anywhere in Italy for a 28 day period and boy did we make the best of it.

Given that the travel costs were reasonable, bearing in mind by the way that I was paid just £120 per month and Pat £100 a month, we decided that we would keep costs down by staying in youth hostels across Italy. It was a big adventure. Neither of us had actually been abroad alone and almost everyone then, like now I suppose, went on an arranged package tour. But after the debacle of Greece it was a no brainer.

We flew to Milan (£55 return). You can get a flight cheaper today half a century on, isn't that remarkable! When we arrived in Milan we stayed in a rather dodgy neighbourhood but what surprised me most was the money. At that time the Lira was the Italian currency but inflation in Italy was so high, far beyond the 15% inflation in the UK; that the Lira actually lost value on a daily basis. On the day after our arrival I went into a shop and bought something with my high denomination travellers cheques. The shopkeeper gave me change along with my purchase and to my horror the change was in telephone tokens.

Filled with British outrage that this foreigner was trying to diddle me I argued with Pat that I should confront him. Just then a friendly local who spoke good English came over to me and explained that the shopkeeper was actually doing me a favour because we were foreigners. The tokens you see would keep their value, a telephone call would cost the same next week and next month but the equivalent Lira would be a fraction of its value by then.

From Milan, where we were frankly shocked by the pornographic magazines on open sale near the Cathedral, we got the train to Venice. We loved it and stayed in a nice Hostel which was on an island opposite St Mark's square and could be accessed via a

vaporetto water taxi. Hostels then of course were single sex dormitory affairs as they were in the UK so it came as no surprise.

We both made ourselves comfortable in a bunk in our respective dormitories and satisfied ourselves with the beautiful view our rooms afforded of the square across the water. It was a bargain. Venice is so romantic and there was so much to see. We spent our time visiting everything we could on our restricted budget and eating pizzas every night (that's where I got the taste for them which has stayed with me to this day).

We left Venice with regret and caught the train to our next stop Florence. Neither of us had any language skills and we found for the first time that on that particular train few Italians at the time spoke English. We travelled second class as you would expect from the price and huddled down for the trip. As we went, there were announcements in Italian for the various stops and I looked anxiously every time to see if we had arrived.

When we eventually got to our destination we nearly missed it altogether. The announcement came that we were approaching Firenze so we ignored it. Suddenly I remembered that this might be Florence. Pat wouldn't have it and insisted it was the wrong stop. It took considerable persuasion to convince her we were there and we just got off in time, throwing our packs to the floor and jumping off as the train began to leave.

We stayed in a large stately home in the hills above Florence and had a good time there especially visiting the Cathedral of Santa Maria Del Fiori. We went up to visit the dome and to my shame I got stuck half way around as I was terrified of heights and had a panic attack because the stone railing was only waist high. I was very embarrassed but Pat, unperturbed helped me carry on, part of the way on my hands and knees, holding up the endless stream of tourists behind me.

The biggest shock I got in Florence though came courtesy of a cup of coffee. One day we had taken our turn around the famous Uffizi Gallery and looked enviously at the posh waiters in the surrounding restaurants we knew we could not afford. Free of our

haversacks we enjoyed the lovely day and decided to visit the cafe on the roof of the Uffizi. It was only a museum cafe after all, like the one on the top story of the Liverpool Museum so we knew we could afford it and drink our coffee in the sunshine enjoying the views over the city. It turned out to be more expensive than we thought. They charged us £5 each for the coffee. An outrageous sum even now which wiped our spending capacity out for that leg of the trip. I'm not sure the coffee was worth it, but the service was good and the views fantastic.

From Florence we caught the Train to Rome and stayed at the hostel in the Olympic Village where I now regularly visit the 6 nations rugby matches at the Stadio Olympico. Rome is today my favourite city in Europe but then I was disappointed. It wasn't a good stop. I had not recovered from the coffee at the Uffizzi and Rome seemed expensive and dirty by comparison with the northern cities. We stayed just one night in the youth hostel which was filled with Arabs I remember or they may have been north African, anyway Pat was harassed by them and I got worried when I was approached by a group who wanted to buy her.

We moved out sharpish and found a tiny one room pensione near the Termini station called the Positano. It was cheap, a bit grubby and in a dodgy area but the people were lovely and it was a relief to get away from the Arabs. We also lost our camera in Rome. It wasn't stolen but on a visit to the catacombs, which we never actually found despite my best efforts I dropped and smashed the camera and all of our pictures from that leg were lost. We were both very upset.

I think we were both glad to leave Rome but we looked forward to our next stop, the Neapolitan coast. This was my favourite part of the trip though I think Pat preferred the north. Sorrento youth hostel was the highlight for me. Run by a typical Italian mama and with glorious weather. It was there I was for the only time in my life the object of female adulation.

A group of Canadian schoolgirls were staying at the hostel and according to Pat who shared their dormitory were convinced I was a Canadian Ice Hockey star and took every chance to gaze lovingly at me. Our trip to Pompeii was also a revelation and has inspired my deep interest in all things Roman ever since. We flew home from Milan and by the time we left after just three weeks the Lira had halved in value against the pound. It was a lively holiday and had cost us very little.

Flushed with the success of Italy we decided to do the same in Holland in the autumn. We bought a return ticket on the ferry from Hull and a good job too as you will read.

We started in Rotterdam. Boring, dirty and industrial, we were glad to leave then on the train, very swish fast and modern to Amsterdam. Amsterdam was more of an education than anything

123

else.  The youth hostel was situated on a canal in the centre of the red light district and we were greeted on arrival with a notice on the door advising us where to buy the best and safest drugs!  Over the next few days we were offered a variety of drugs from dealers around the tourist areas and were frankly shocked.  We were even more shocked at the wide ranging choice of prostitutes sitting behind their individual shop windows.  I will always remember one lady who was so striking if that is the correct word that we took a detour every day to see a sight we could not believe.  The lady was Asian, probably Indonesian I guess, about fifty years old and heavy but wearing nothing but a mini dress made entirely from bright blue string!!!

**Priceless**

This biggest problem with Amsterdam though was the cost.  We were due to say for several days but completely ran out of money and had to move on early.  Our next two stops in Grou and Leeuwarden in the north were a relief as we looked around the lovely old Frisian towns but then we had to move to the island of Texel as the Frisian youth hostels were full and we couldn't extend.  We weren't looking forward to Texel and it had been an unknown quantity when I booked it but it turned out to be the highlight of the holiday.

By the time we got to Texel we had no money at all but had fortunately pre-paid the hostel.  We spent the days on the beach enjoying the cold strong sun.  The beaches are as good as any in the Caribbean.  We had no money to buy food so during the day we obtained milk straight from the cows at local farmhouses and spent the morning picking blackberries which we ate for our dinner with the fresh milk.  My dad always told me to carry an emergency pack of Kendal mint cake and OXO cubes, a thing he learned in the army.

The advice proved invaluable. As we sat in the hostel and made our OXOs for our evening meal other sympathetic hostellers gave us their left-over vegetables to add to our makeshift gravy.

On the last day we walked to the rail station, there is a railway bridge over to Texel island. We still had our return ticket so were able to get back to Hull but when we arrived we had no more cash to get home so I went, warrant card in hand to the British Transport Police and got a travel warrant to get back to Lime Street in Liverpool. Im not sure that is still possible to do now but it was a different world then. It was certainly an interesting trip and another learning experience.

We had been engaged now for a couple of years and we had set the date at last for July 1978. in the Sefton General Hospital nurses home, I wasn't allowed inside and there was a woman in the foyer called the 'Home Sister' who enforced this rigidly so when I went to see her we could only sit in the shared sitting room near the front entrance but I had to be out by 11 pm. On many occasions I would miss the last bus as we said our goodbyes and I would 'tab' the 6 miles home in the early hours, but I was fit then and I walked a lot further at work every day.

Eventually Pat decided to join a group of friends and they rented a tiny flat over a shop on Smithdown Road a few hundred yards away from the Hospital and we were able to spend time together there depending on our shifts. I'd turn up on my motorbike and we managed to see each other two or three times a week. Our transport consisted of my Honda 250cc motorbike which was underpowered really but got us around. We agreed that we would put one salary away toward buying a house and getting married so lived on £50 a month each. Out of this I ran the motorbike and Pat paid for her room.

On 7th July 1978, we stepped out of All Saints Church, Oakfield, Anfield, man and wife, married by a priest who was only a few years

older than me! Prior to the wedding we were required to go to marriage 'lessons' delivered by the same priest to ensure we were spiritually and morally prepared. When we started the lessons we began to question the priest.

Father Newnes was his name asked Pat which school she went to and when she told him Broughton Hall he scoffed at their naive liberality. He then asked me and when I told him SFX under the Jesuits he almost paled and said, - *'Oh well you won't need this then'*

It was a special day, of course. I paid for the car and flowers, Pat's dad for everything else. We'd already confirmed privately to each other that we wanted to spend our lives together. In a way, the wedding day was almost the formal confirmation of that. In those days weddings were the parent's affair. They determined who it was correct to invite and arrangements had to be agreed with them. These days parents are almost incidental and have less to do with making the arrangements but simply provide the bulk of the cash. This means that in 1978 our wedding was primarily a family affair and the bulk of the guests were aunts uncles and cousins.

While the ceremony and wedding reception was more family than friends. We had more scope to invite friends to the evening 'Do'. A few of my friends from school attended, more of Pat's friends but by 1978 I had moved on and the bulk of the people I invited were friends from Huyton. Bob (the man with the rat) was my best man and

another friend Steve whose beat had been adjacent to mine for some time, together with their girlfriends came to the wedding breakfast.

We had the evening 'Do' at a function hall called the 'Tudor Rooms' on Kensington near Old Swan where my nan and Grandad Gill had lived when I was a child. For its time our wedding was a lavish affair but it was still quite traditional in the way it was conducted and much more formal than nowadays. Pat's family sort of sat together at one side of the hall and my family at the other side mixing was not extensive. I must admit that I fully expected the wedding to end in the usual large scale disturbance if someone took real or imagined offence. This was not uncommon at Scouse weddings of the time. My precautions were I think successful and many who attended later told me and Pat that it was the best wedding they had ever attended. I must say Mr McLoughlin did us proud.

At the end of the evening as is traditional we made our farewells and set off to our new house in St Helens. Steve and his girlfriend gave us a lift and we left the revellers to go home in their own time or when the Tudor Room staff threw them out. Like everyone else at the time it was difficult to get time together when you are courting and both Steve and his girlfriend Jackie who he had met at a brew spec in

Page Moss had families who were unwilling to leave them on their own. I think that they saw an opportunity to stay with us overnight. They would not leave! Unfortunately we had other ideas and a heavy cold into the bargain and just wanted to be on our own on our wedding night.

Our house was on a newly built estate in a place called Laffak in St Helens. It cost £9,600, and we'd saved up a £1,200 deposit. We actually bought it the year before we got married so we could decorate it to suit ourselves and collect enough furniture for our new life. Whenever I smell turpentine, I think of this time because we spent those first six months sanding down and varnishing tables, chairs, bookcases and so on. I was the first in my family to own, not rent a

house. But that's more than OK: I would go on to achieve a good many more family firsts as my life moved along.

We had chosen St Helens really because the houses were a lot cheaper, it was after all the back of beyond, or so we thought at the time, says he living in a farm house in deepest Wales. It was problematic for work though. We only had our single motorbike and when we were first married Pat still worked in Sefton General and I was at Huyton. Whilst I used the bike (Pat couldn't drive a car and wouldn't drive a motorbike) so she had to walk two miles every morning to catch a two hour bus ride into Liverpool. Some sacrifice I may say. Occasionally, if she was late or missed the bus and I was able, I would take her on the motorbike to Huyton Railway Station and she would get a train or bus the rest of the way.

One day as a wind up I dropped her off at 6am and immediately after parade I went with Bob in the Police car and shouted at the other people at the bus stop that she was a dangerous escaped mental patient and they should keep back while I bundled her and her motorbike helmet into the Police car and then took her to work. She was mortified but grateful for the lift I think.

One of the first things we did when we got married was to build our family and that meant getting a dog, or rather two dogs. We first saw an advert for a border collie pup in Wallasey Wirral. We set out on our motorbike and bought the black and white ball of fur for just £15. Pat put it into her backpack and we took it home and called it Bonnie because it looked fat and healthy but it turned out the fatness was due to worms. After we wormed it, it returned to a normal puppy size.

Pat wanted a Labrador as well though and we eventually saw one for sale in Halewood. Again we went on the motorbike and took it home in our backpack. This time we paid pedigree prices and Sophie as we called her cost us £65. A not inconsiderable sum even today.

We loved both dogs but Sophie was a typical Labrador and became very destructive when we were both at work. One day we came home to find her lying on her side in the kitchen, her stomach was the same size as the rest of her body. She had broken into the fridge and eaten her own weight in frozen dog food.

After that I bought a wooden shed so she could not damage the doors and skirting board which I had already replaced on several occasions. The shed lasted less than a week as she ate a large hole in the wall and escaped. I gave up. We eventually came to the sad conclusion that she was just too boisterous and destructive to stay alone in a house where both people worked and we looked to re-home her.

I spoke to a dog handler who suggested she might make a drugs dog. We tearfully took her to the dog section and handed her to the Inspector where she was named Pepper after the heroine of the 'Policewoman' series then on the TV. Weeks later they returned her to us. She had failed the course. Her sniffing skills were first class but she was terrified of loud noises and thus of no practical use as a Police Dog. In desperation we asked Mr McLoughlin if she could stay with him for a few weeks till we could find a new home but he fell in love with her and treated her as his child for the rest of her life.

As soon as I finished my probation I was put on the list for a driving course. I was lucky that the police taught me to drive from scratch and it took just 6 weeks to bring me up to Police pursuit driving standard. It didn't mean that I got a car beat but I was a spare driver for reliefs so I did manage to get out of the rain occasionally. Once I could drive I needed a car but we didn't have much money to buy one. There was a garage though at one of the extremities of my beat and one night in the very early hours I spotted a new car for the same price as an old banger. I mentally debated for several weeks and the car was still there when I got my full licence. So I went in and bought it, a red Citroen CV6 complete with starting handle! I was very pleased but soon found out why it was so cheap as it was rather idiosyncratic both to start and to drive. The roll-back rubber roof was lovely in the sun but leaked when it rained and it was practically impossible to find a mechanic who could work on it so I had to learn to do things myself and I have never been the most practical of men.

Now that we had a car (however temperamental) we decided to take a belated honeymoon in the summer of 1979. We set off to the South Coast and toured Hampshire, Dorset, Wiltshire, Devon and Cornwall staying in Bed and Breakfast accommodation. Somehow our car held up even though on the steep hill into Truro my accelerator pedal detached from the cable and I found myself having to switch off the engine and coast to a panicked halt but apart from that and a very leaky roof we had a lovely time and got home in one piece. Two of us set out, we didn't know it but three of us came back.

I knew very early on that policing and I were a great fit. It combined freedom, power and camaraderie. From the downside of working night shifts came the freedom of being outdoors and mile upon mile of silence. From the busyness of days came the buzz of curiosity and working in a team. When you are in the police and you

135

see someone or something of interest, you can go ahead and check it out. No one will stop you.

When I joined, you could progress fast if you were determined to do so. In order to do so though you needed to pass two exams to 'buy a ticket for the selection raffle.' There was then a Sergeant's examination held every November for any officer not in his probation. Anyone who passed this (notified the following February) could immediately sit the Inspector's exam in the April. At the time this exam was not restricted to Sergeants only. In my position, I had not been out of the studying way that long and, once started it was easier to go for both in quick succession, so I did. By my wedding day then I had sat and passed both exams. Not only that but I had passed 2nd in the force and in the top two hundred in the country which gave me an automatic shot at accelerated promotion. Unfortunately I had no 'minders' to coach me and no experience at sitting interviews.

When I applied I had to say what my hobbies were. I had none of course except Pat so I said 'military history'. I attended the interview panel just over a month before my wedding. Brushed up and polished I had this naive belief that my natural brilliance would shine through. A career and a lifetime later I can see what they were looking for and that I didn't have it but at the time I was just disappointed that I went no further. Despite this, even qualifying for the interview did me good hence the driving course following rapidly, and less than a year later a move to Kirkby Station as an acting Sergeant. By then though I had been approached by one of the Huyton Inspectors Eric who was moving to the Operational Support Division (OSD) and I set my sight on this as my next chapter.

Pat finished her Nurse Training, had done exceptionally well and been offered a plum job as a cardiac nursing specialist at Sefton General. Given our new home though she opted to move to Billinge which was relatively close to St Helens and begin a midwifery course.

# St Anne Street Blues

**'Take a look at the lawman,
beating up the wrong guy.
Oh man,
wonder if he'll ever know
he's in the best-selling show.
Is there life on Mars?'**
(Life on Mars TV Theme – David Bowie)

 The old Frank Sinatra song, My Way has a line in it,

*'Regrets, I've had a few, but then again too few to mention.'*

Well I could sing a version of that about Friends. I've had a few but then again too few to mention. Apart from Pat and my own family, I have had few close and lasting friends. At school I had just a handful and when I joined the Police a handful too but maybe the job of a policeman doesn't help.

It didn't take me long to work out that, whilst most people are pleased when police turn up in emergencies, few want you as their friend. Even family treated me differently. That long ago killing by my great-great-grandfather aside, both sides of my family seem generally to have been regular, law-abiding folk. Even so.

Once I had actually decided to join I mentioned it to my mum and dad. Dad was supportive of my decision though I suspect he may have wanted me to go to university but my mum's reaction was,

*"What do you want to do that for, I thought you would make something of yourself."*

I suppose this betrayed some fear, suspicion, hostility to the Police and maybe was even a function of her family's 'Feinian' leanings.

I notice fewer invitations come our way. When I speak to my aunties and uncles I find them more guarded and find it odd. The same thing is true of Pat's family though few say anything openly, years later, just before I retire Pat goes to her uncle's funeral and overhears an uncle saying,

*'Well I never thought our Trish would marry a copper".* Betraying the underlying antipathy toward the Police I suspect. What is it that they think I would discover? Or do to them?

I remember going to my Uncle Billy's funeral (my mum's brother) in 1979 in Frodsham. Billy and his wife Elsie were terribly respectable but the whole family were there in Billy's small cottage when another uncle suddenly launched into an attack on the Police and by implication me. It was unexpected and unpleasant and really

141

got my hackles up. The others said nothing but I could see that this was the prevailing family opinion. The only exception to this was my aunty Emma and her family who welcomed me almost on a daily basis to her house which I made a regular brew spec on my beat and plied me with tea and cakes without demur.

I got nothing but pride and support from the Gills but even so there was a similar suspicion I suppose you could call it from Nan's wider family who were never actually hostile but noticeably uncomfortable and guarded when they spoke to me, a marked difference in tone from before I joined.

But to be fair, maybe I myself was at least partly to blame. At times, it is me who has to step back. My friend Wally who had attended my engagement 'do' at the Police club invited us to a student party at a big house in Sefton Park. Before we got to the porch, we smelt what could have been petuli oil or could have been cannabis. We never stayed long to find out.

Pat's friend Margaret invited us to a party at her new flat not long after I joined. I do remember that there were a lot of snide comments about my job. Margaret was Pat's best friend and they were very close but she grew more and more distant quite quickly and I attribute this to my being a policeman.

It can be isolating turning away from friends or family 'just in case' or feeling uncomfortable that they can't relax their guard (about goodness knows what) when you are around. Instead, like most

142

people within the force, we began mixing solely with other officers and their partners and spouses. OK for me, but restrictive for Pat.

This isolation was recognised with the growth of 'protected' social spaces. There had been a Police Club for many years. There was a tendency to arrange socials at this venue where few outsiders were present. In the late seventies each police station started to include a bar and social club space which really reflected the sense of 'otherness' that the police family felt. Increasingly isolated and rejected by normal society friends and even wider family. We almost felt like an army of occupation at times.

For me and Pat the isolation was exaggerated even more at quite an early stage. I got the opportunity to be acting sergeant when the post-holder at Kirkby Police station was on extended sick leave. Technically I was posted to a car beat but in practice I became the Acting Street Sergeant on 3 scale at Kirkby which consisted of three cars and six foot patrols.

Kirkby was by this time a more settled place than it had been when I was a baby but it still carried its notorious reputation, no longer really applicable when you got under its skin though. I was twenty two years old, and not everyone had taken kindly to being held accountable to someone this young.

I wasn't one of the boys – because I was at sergeant level. I wasn't one of the bosses because I was 'acting' the rank temporarily ahead of other, more street-experienced officers who had not sat their exams and resented me.

Eric had been my Inspector at Huyton since I started there in 1976 and had been impressed with my work rate and the fact that I had the reputation as someone who was 'clean'. Many officers had a reputation for drinking, malingering and having too many romances so to speak whilst on duty. Other officers were compromised by 'friends' in the Freemasons or suspected of taking pay-offs for charges to be dropped. I was regarded as a bit 'straight'. Didn't drink much, (it made me sick), and I didn't womanise, (I was getting married). As a Catholic I was contemptuous of secret societies and I was fiercely against those on the 'take'. I had famously had a serious disagreement with a bobby who approached me on the stairwell one day and asked me to drop charges against a friend of his, pointing out that it could be in my financial and career interest to do so. I had kicked off seriously and publicly and threatened to arrest him for perverting the course of justice if he pushed it. The argument became a matter of great interest and amusement in some circles and I was told that it was a mistake to push back against the tide but such warnings had no effect on me.

Liverpool has a history of violent, organised criminal activity that dates back to Victorian times. Over the years, robust policing would knock it back – then up it would re-emerge. Merseyside was a bad place in the late 70's and Liverpool especially violent and crime ridden.

There was a history of 'Special Squads' being formed. The Commandos in the late 60's were a detective squad of ex military men who after cleaning up organised crime (reputedly the Krays feared to come to Liverpool) the Commandos took to organising it themselves. They were followed by the 'Task Force' a popular name reflected in the TV drama 'Softly Softly Task Force', a spin off from Z Cars.

Where the Commandos were plain clothes detectives the Task Force were a uniform body and drove around in Landrovers with a mission to eradicate public disorder. These were of course the very same 'Jeeps' that Sgt Harrop warned me of. In fact the Jeeps had such a reputation that I remember when working in the Library I was warned to keep out of sight if a Jeep was around for fear of being picked up and subject to random casual violence, whether I was guilty of anything or not.

By 1979 the Task Force reputation for casual violence was accompanied by members hiring themselves out as 'Bouncers' and for excessive hard drinking. The Chief Constable decided to try again hence the formation of the OSD made up of one hundred and twenty officers split into fifteen units of six Constables and a Sergeant. A new Superintendent Mike Prunty, a Chief Inspector Peter Smith and five Inspectors (including Eric) all of whom were known as rather straight laced and free from scandal were brought in to head the unit and recruit new people of a similar profile. I fitted that description.

So after just a couple of months at Kirkby I was posted to the OSD based in St. Anne Street Police Station in Liverpool city centre.

Just as in the police TV drama Hill Street Blues which first aired in January 1981, life in the OSD was a sweet and sour mix of high, fast drama plus stand-offs and successes. I watched it keenly. Despite a

Chicago setting, it remains to this day the most realistic drama on policing I have seen.

In terms of career progression, enjoying a squeaky-clean reputation led to an exceptional opportunity. In 1979, the Operational Support Division was a new, elite cohort of officers who had impeccable records and had demonstrated consistent initiative in their day-to-day policing work. It was the unit I'd wanted to be part of the minute I'd learnt about it. You had to be asked. I had only been a police officer for five minutes, so I was humbled to be approached.

Officially, the job covered two main roles. One was to police public disorder – when you'd wear a uniform. The second was to be part of a fast, effective anti-street-crime patrol– when you'd be in plain clothes and driving unmarked vehicles. Mark 2 Ford Cortinas and Mark 1 Vauxhall Cavaliers, the successors of the Z cars of old, and very fast. The Cortina's were better on the straight but wallowed badly on corners with their soft suspension.

The Cavaliers were better, faster and more manoeuvrable but they had a flat spot when entering second gear that proved at times to be crucial when chasing fast cars.

In lay language, our job was to 'clean up the city'. And clean it up we did! During my time with the OSD, we forced crime and disorder right down by making a tremendous number of arrests. Bringing down vehicle crime was our greatest success. Car crime was the number one crime then, cars were easy to steal and provided excitement for the young criminal.

Once I chased down a Rolls Royce which was the most expensive car I had caught, another night we received a report of a stolen Ferrari. Within second there it was just yards in front of me. This was a time that I needed everything the Police Car had; but the Cavalier's weak spot proved decisive. Before I could change up to third gear the Ferrari was out of sight and lost.

The drawbacks of the Cortina though nearly led to my downfall another night. I picked up a stolen car near a set of tenements called Thomas White Gardens and my passenger was providing a

commentary of the chase over open radio. The stolen car headed into a cul-de-sac and I cried out that we had him only to see the car mount a kerb ahead and sail through the middle of two concrete bollards. I put my foot down and headed for the middle of the posts.

Unfortunately the Cortina was about two inches wider than the stolen car and I got wedged between. Embarrassing as the whole force could hear my discomfort and cursing on the open radio channel. I was mildly reprimanded but little else. My record and reputation saved me.

A few years later I did something similar with a new Personnel carrier in the early hours of the morning. A change in design meant the new vehicles had protruding rear wheel arches and I took one off against a bollard. My sergeant came to my aid that night and we had the car fixed at a garage he knew by the time we went off duty (though the respray wasn't quite dry. The next night on parade, the Chief Inspector gave everyone their duties and finished by saying. *'Can whoever got the new Personnel carrier resprayed, please make sure next time the paint shade matches.'*

## We never flinched

On the beat, I'd had my twenty arrests a month target. On the OSD, I would be charging four or more villains every shift. Stop and Search was a leading tool because it worked. Thieves carried large bunches of car keys fitting every type of car. Robbers had knives. We policed the ghetto areas of town harshly. Maybe this contributed in some ways to the riots a few years later. Yet our actions were needed because these areas teemed with criminals and it was really dangerous for ordinary people to walk the streets safely.

We policed public order events, arriving at speed in personnel carriers. Our aim to stop trouble in its tracks was mostly achieved. My

149

experience with the rolling pub fights was writ large in the city centre but within two years the city centre was a quieter safer place though police on the periphery continued to battle away. When a particular part of the city reached crisis point we were deployed there temporarily to restore some normality and things usually returned to normal by the time we left.

With so many court cases ongoing as a result of the high arrest levels, it was vital an OSD officer was top of his game. Off duty, you weren't allowed to go into the city centre. If you came on duty and there was the smell of alcohol on your breath – that was the end of you and the OSD. The regime was so intense that a rule was made that smelling of mints (often used to mask the smell of alcohol) would be enough to be sent back to your division. I didn't drink, so that was no problem – or at least not until I accepted a six-month secondment to CID. But more of that later.

I started well in the OSD. I was paired with a lad called Mike who, although I didn't know it at the time lived in the same street as Pat. Mike was very straight and quite moralistic but oddly I got on with him well immediately. He looked like Inspector Clouseau and had the smelliest feet in the world enclosed in Chelsea boots which I'm sure he never removed for the two years I worked with him.

On our first day we were told to wait around as is usual in new jobs but we quickly completed our admin and got bored. We told our new sergeant, (call me Dave! That was new) that we would go for a walk so he told us to just keep out of trouble. We had walked just half a mile from the station when we spotted what we both saw as a suspicious car. What we found established our legend from the off, a whole bag of stolen credit cards and jewellery. A good start indeed.

The sense of otherness that the Police felt within the community was mirrored to some extent in the relationship between the OSD and the rest of the force. Friends you had only weeks earlier in the Division were less friendly when you were a member of the OSD. This was partly a jealousy issue I suspect but we were also the Unit of first resort when it came to dealing with internal corruption.

Within weeks of my posting my unit was given the task of keeping covert observations on a set of shops in Birkenhead where the local Police section were suspected of undertaking a series of shop burglaries during the night shift. Only the divisional Chief Superintendent knew we were there and we couldn't tell the local Inspector who was also under suspicion. Eventually our cover was blown and our command and the Division had a big bust up with us in the middle. Very uncomfortable and not something that endeared us to the rest of the force.

One night we were called in early and told that we were to mount a raid on a Police Social event in Huyton at which some illegal pornography was suspected. Again we were expected to be the enforcers and it was uncomfortable to arrest a number of my former mates, even though fortunately none were from my own former shift.

I'd become a firearms officer by this point, and it's on a joint OSD and CID operation that I came the closest in my career to shooting someone.

Typically, there are three reasons to carry arms.

• One, an immediate threat to life using a weapon.

• Two, as part of a high risk escort. I regularly formed part of the convoy that escorted 80 million pounds of used bank notes from the Bank of England premises in Liverpool to the Bank of England in Manchester to be destroyed.

• Three, a major crime involving firearms.

In this case a taxi driver had been robbed at gunpoint, and the suspect was believed to be hiding in a flat on the fifth floor of a tower block, Entwistle Heights Toxteth.

*'Wait by the lift, Lenny,'* I was ordered. *'If anyone comes out the flat – it'll be the suspect. He'll be armed, so shoot the bastard.'*

**'Freeze. Armed police!'**

I say the words I have been trained to use – and thank goodness I do. The man coming full pelt toward me is only visible as a silhouette and has a gun in his hand – time slows down. To pull the trigger, or not?

'Don't shoot, don't shoot, CID, CID', a detective had exited the flat over the balcony to search the drying area. What an idiot.

Why didn't I shoot, Procedures. Training. It's there for a reason.

I said that I didn't drink, and that was a positive advantage in the OSD but it became a problem, big time when I was selected to do a stint in the CID at Speke who like all the CID in Merseyside had an appalling reputation for heavy drinking and was a deeply entrenched culture protected by many at the highest levels of the Force.

It was summer 1980, and by then, I'd become a father to Lenny. It meant that, whilst I was ready to give 110% to my work, I didn't want to be sitting in pubs with colleagues until 3 a.m. I also felt uncomfortable that some of those hours were being put down as overtime – despite my boss, arguably the keenest drinker, being in no fit state to tell a criminal from a chief constable during those so called 'on-call' hours where we were supposedly gathering 'vital intelligence'!

That, however, was the CID culture of the time. Life on Mars, a recent TV drama set in 1973, shows this crass, second-rate state of affairs very nicely.

I stood my ground: I went soberly home to my wife at the official end of each shift. And when I saw corruption, I challenged it head-on.

*'Come on we're going down to the Somali Club for a few drinks,'* was the call at 11pm at least three nights every week (after working since 9am!)

*'No thanks, I've got a wife and baby to go home to.'* I would say after the first couple of visits had demonstrated to me the waste of time this was.

*'You'll never get into the CID permanently if you don't come out with us and be one of the lads.'*

*'Fine by me,'* I would say and go home.

Once, I was asked to falsify a burglary report. I'd been called to a butcher's shop where several sides of beef had gone missing overnight.

*'It was stolen in a burglary,'* I told my sergeant.

*'You don't know that,'* came the reply. *'I think storm damage could have blown a hole in the roof. So not a break-in. Can you adjust the report?'*

When I refused, he sent a different officer back to reassess the scene. The purpose of the lie? It had been about reducing crime figures. The sergeant had known that it was hugely unlikely the thief would be caught – the meat would have been sold on by now. Denying that a crime had taken place was a sure-fire way to reduce the unsolved crime records. The number of Tax Discs that were mysteriously blown away from car windscreens by high winds must have necessitated a change in design surely!

My final straw was witnessing a fellow experienced detective so drunk that he couldn't coherently conduct an interview with a suspected paedophile. That man had been drinking for more than six hours forgetting he had 'warned in for interview' a suspect in a child-abuse case. After ten minutes, I couldn't bear it anymore – I interrupted the detective who was really a lot more senior than me and told the suspect to go home. We would be in touch on another day. I'm not sure whether my colleague actually noticed the man had gone.

Thirty minutes later, he turned around in his swivel chair, suddenly apparently sober.

*'It's nine o'clock son, get your coat on and well go for a pint,'*
he said

Despite my protest he almost dragged me out to the pub opposite the nick which was managed by a famous retired ex-boxer. Within minutes my colleague had picked a fight with the landlord, and, deciding that discretion was the better part of valour I dragged him back to the nick before tempers frayed and fists flew. An extreme example – yes. But this truly was how it was in 1980's Liverpool.

After six months I had to decide what to do, stay or return to the OSD. I'm sure you can guess what I did. It didn't do my career any good to walk away from CID after those six miserable months. But I had no regrets. Whiter than white and the OSD, that was policing my style.

So back I went. Back to a new Unit led by Sergeant, Dickie. The best Sergeant I ever had and within months everything changed forever.

# When the Going Gets Tough, the Tough Get Going

**'If you can wait and not be tired by waiting**
**Or being lied about, don't deal in lies**
**Or being hated, don't give way to hating**
**And yet don't look too good, nor talk too wise.'**
('If' – Rudyard Kipling)

*'One X Ray 6 from CH. Can you return to St Anne Street immediately. We need everyone to change into uniform – there's been a bit of trouble in Toxteth.'*

I'm back in the OSD when I hear these orders. I am back at the sharp end. It is not a total surprise, the area has been starting to bubble like a kettle does before it boils, getting noisier and more agitated for more than a week now.

We paraded on at 6pm, and were deployed to B Division, looking for stolen cars in X Ray 6 and X Ray 7 (our call signs). It is now nearly midnight and we curse, there's a lot of activity tonight in Norris Green and a good chance of a late arrest and overtime. Better than sitting in St Anne St playing cards waiting for nothing to happen.

Dickie, walks in from a meeting with Gerry the Inspector and tells us to hurry up, we are going to patrol town and hopefully pick up a couple of jobs outside the clubs, no-one thinks that Toxteth will pop tonight even though there was an incident earlier where another Gerry and his unit were attacked by a mob in Granby St when they arrested a lad on a motorbike, Gerry is in hospital. But we can but hope!

We mounted up, allocated a long wheelbase Personnel Carrier X Ray 17. Mike driving; Dick in the front seat; then a jostle for places in the back. The idea is to be nearest the side door, then you're first or second out at a job and can bag the prisoner, no prize for tardiness here. It's a competition, three pairs. Mike and Ray (sharp, aggressive and top so far this month but its still only the 7th). Me and Peter my new partner and to this day one of my few close friends. Tony and his partner 'Animal', neither too bright but full of bluster. I always did my best to be last in, next to the door with control over the handle while Peter tucked in by the window and was rarely first, or even third out (far too nice to deny the others).

Tonight I delay as we get in so I can claim my usual seat by the door but Ray tells me, *'Nope. Not moving, You'll have to climb over!'*, I clamber over him, annoyed to sit between him and Peter and leave him in pole position. I'm lucky he doesn't give me a dig. We head into town, it's hot tonight and the van is steamy and airless. We are in uniform and all have our riot bags with us with extra equipment so there is little room left. The pubs have let out and people are heading for the nightclubs. Between midnight and 2am is a bit of a lull though. so we still have time. We choose Victoria Street outside the 'She' club, always worth a punt and with the added chance of a nonce coming out of the fairy glen (an underground gent's toilet opposite). It's boring now, we hear chatter on the radio about stones being

159

thrown in Toxteth but nothing serious and we have been told to give it a wide berth anyway.

Its' almost 2am, no prisoners and the chances of overtime are dwindling fast. Suddenly:

*'Any patrol Victoria street stolen vehicle registered number..... '*

And there it is, in all its beautiful glory speeding past us toward the Gyratory, Mike takes off, Dick puts on the lights and off we go.

Only yards and it's turning into the Haymarket, and its stalling!, bunny hopping toward a stop, a sitting duck, one occupant, an easy take.

Ray, sitting where I should be, opens the sliding side door and jumps out approaching the car now almost stationary and still bunny hopping. I curse him and edge over to follow, it will be his and Mike's overtime and not much time left now for the rest of us.

I'm going after him anyway, and as my feet touch the road surface, Ray is reaching in to take the keys out of the ignition but the car takes off again; he's still trying to get the keys and running alongside now, Animal drags me back inside and we follow, there's other cars arriving and a cacophony of horns blaring, the whole OSD group are joining the chase, Tally Ho!

But, what's he playing at, he's halfway through the window now and his legs are off the ground, Christ the car is accelerating and heading for, No, No, No, the glass bus shelter and he is wiped off on the steel upright as the car crashes into the glass and finally stops.

The whole incident from the 'She' club to the bus stop lasted almost 3 minutes. Ray is effectively dead at the scene and pronounced so less than half an hour later with catastrophic internal injuries. It could have been me. It should have been me, but I suspect I wouldn't have tried to grab the keys, who knows.

When the battered and bloodied driver is eventually carried away in an ambulance and Ray in another ambulance Gerry the Inspector orders us back to St Anne Street for a debrief. We go to the 24 hour canteen and sit, shocked stunned, quiet.

By the time we are interviewed it is mid morning, Ray is dead, a murder enquiry is in full flow and all else is forgotten for now. We are eventually released just after midday and told to get some sleep. I drive zombie like back to Mrs McLoughlin's house where Pat and the

161

baby are staying for the weekend.  Straight to bed, it's 2pm and I remember no more.

It's 3.30 pm and Pat is shaking me awake.  There's someone on the phone downstairs from work. I stumble bleary eyed and take the handset.

*'Parade at 4pm, Toxteth has kicked off.....Sorry.'*

By 6.15pm I and 75 of my colleagues are in a windowless parade room in Wavertree Road Police Station, 500 yards away from Toxteth.  Waiting.  Tired, worried, shocked and excited.

It was July 7th 1981. The Toxteth riots had begun. At the start of this book, I have detailed what happened during what still feels like

'the most frightening time of my life'. Suffice to add, the police on
duty were the only people who could stop the rioters, and we very
nearly didn't.

After the initial riots during the second week of July, there was a
breather of sorts but the atmosphere remained ominous and
oppressive like waiting for a thunder storm to break. The weekend of
the Royal Wedding between Prince Charles and Lady Diana passed
and the day after the wedding it was, ding-ding round two.

Of our Unit, Ray was replaced by Brian who I joined with in 1975.
Animal was hospitalised the first night of the first riots for the
duration and never came back. He was replace a few days later by
Stan. Tony was injured and hospitalised but signed himself out twice
and came back only to be injured again. The man was a lunatic.

Mike was Ray's best friend and never really recovered but stayed as our driver for the rest of the riots. Peter; well Peter slept through most of it. The 'Nodding Dog' we called him. He was amazing. He slept, helmet on, head resting against the plastic inner window of the personnel carrier while petrol bombs and rocks smashed against the outside, millimetres from his head. He had a very useful skill though, he was good at electronics.

I can't speak highly enough of Dickie our Sergeant. He was of the Commando generation and hard as nails but he kept us together, partly through shared adversity but also by some frankly weird traits. Dick loved to suck a lemon on parade and he had an interest in the German army of the second world war which bordered on obsession. He suggested to Peter that he rig up a tape recorder to the Personnel carrier Tannoy system and music blared out as we drove along like Oddball's Tank in the film 'Kelly's Heroes'.

Our favourite was of course Wagner's 'Ride of the Valkyries' after the helicopter scene in 'Apocalypse Now' though Dickie insisted that we play stirring German World War Two songs too from his private collection.

To go with our music Mike got his wife to make a pennant to fly from our antenna like the WW2 tanks have in 'A bridge too far'. Within days these became so popular that every OSD vehicle had them and one was made for the Chief Inspector and Superintendent as well. Until the Chief Constable found out that is.

Towards the end, when the Personnel Carriers were so battered despite solid tyres and newly made grills on the windows we reverted once more to the 'Jeeps' of old which still had a strange psychological effect on the 'enemy'. Paint bombs followed so the garage fitted windscreen washers filled with turps and the sides were re-inforced with solid steel armour. Despite this Brian is hit in the back with a metal railing clean through the plate but is saved by his personal body armour, an innovation newly introduced to us.

By the second week of August the rain has arrived, the heat of July has subsided and the rioters have exhausted themselves, and us. We hand over day to day policing of Toxteth to the foot patrols drawn from many forces and we in the OSD retire to recuperate in the peripheral divisions.

We at last have time to reflect and in some senses grieve, and Ray Davenport is eventually laid to rest as those of us still standing from our unit act as pall bearers at his funeral with full Police honours.

My promotion to sergeant came in September 1981, just two months after the riots and it threw me into a firing line of a different sort: hostile subordinates. I stepped away from the OSD to take the promotion back at Huyton. Some of the officers I was given to supervise were sound but a few were simply lazy and others positively malicious.

166

My new Inspector Tommy was an old barrel like detective who walked like a seaman with a rolling gait. His nick name was 'Ann-Ann', nothing to do with the panda of that name but because of his tendency to start his sentences, '*an-an-an-an.......*'

He greeted me when I arrived as an old friend though I didn't know him. He told me that I should have been awarded the George Medal and he was glad to have me. Tommy was a bobbies boss and saw his job to protect those under his command. He was well liked and effective but had a tendency to ignore bad apples or give them the benefit of the doubt a bit too much.

The senior man on the shift was Trefor, a surly, untidy mountain of a welshman who I had known when I was a Constable and he had been the car driver in Halewood. Trefor was a slob and married to the canteen supervisor who bullied him unmercifully and to whom he was a mouse. To the rest of the world however he was bad tempered and someone who you would not want to pick a fight with as you wouldn't get up again. Trefor was a problem or so I thought.

The other big problem was one of the response car drivers who was similarly dirty and slovenly but more snide than dangerous. He openly disagreed with me on parade and showed contempt, disappearing off the grid with monotonous regularity but always with a transparent excuse that I could never disprove. Always sailing close to the wind but never in a way I could punish without damaging myself and appearing weak. Tommy, bless him was no help but in the end Trefor was the answer.

In St Columba's I was a house captain (prefect). In such a rough school there were people you didn't cross, even at that age. I

167

befriended a big, rather dim, heavy called Bev who acted as my minder and enforcer, I never had any problem with even the roughest kids.

Well I recruited Trefor in a similar role. Every man has his key and Trefor wanted responsibility. He was overlooked and ignored because he was surly and scruffy but was a clever man. He saw lots, said little and had shed-loads of experience. I bared my soul to Trefor as an old colleague I had looked up to when I was a recruit. He responded with advice and I made him my acting Sergeant and confidant to cover on my rest days or when I covered the Bridewell. He was after all the senior man even if he hadn't ever passed the exam and it was after all my decision and Tommy backed me up.

While intimidation was mostly effective, luck also played a part (after all God helps those who help themselves they say). A vacancy arose in the Plain Clothes Department who deal with vice and licensing. Tommy suggested that I recommend my remaining problem for the job. I had a moral problem with this but he convinced me it was a good solution. Make the man someone else's problem. I agreed.

With a combination of intimidation and guile I had gained total control of the section. It was a useful lesson and one I would repeat more than once in my career.

And what of the man in plain clothes. Well he eventually became an Inspector in Training. Very correct, very smart. I met him years later and he greeted me enthusiastically and thanked me for the favour I did him all those years ago which got him out of his self imposed rut, changed his career and his life. Lessons all round then.

What of Trefor you may ask, well I helped him pass his Sergeants exam and he got promoted shortly before he retired and thus got a better pension. I think he and Elsie stayed together. God makes some people and matches them.

Once I had control, the section's work rate and reputation improved. It even survived the arrival of another Sergeant transferred from Traffic for a disciplinary offence and marking time till retirement. We called him the Sand-Dancer. He was very tall and very thin and looked like the old music hall act Wilson, Keppel and Betty. See the video of them below.

**Https://www.youtube.com/watch?v=Sn83cCEpZVO**

A year later Tommy and I were asked to go and sort out the Day and Evening Patrol section at Eaton Road (Days and EPs for short) which was now in the same Division as Huyton. The Days and Evening Patrol Section should have been the Divisional OSD but they were a disorganised drunken mess conducting a regime of petty crime. The former Sergeant and Inspector were ineffectual and bullied by the men who were all old sweats and set in their ways. Not averse to intimidation.

*'You'll have to watch out with your car,'* I was told by one of the older men,

*'What do you mean by that'*, I said.

*'Well Sarge, there are some bad people working here and you have to have eyes in the back of you're head'*

169

What this meant of course was that they would tamper with my car
– to keep myself alive even, I would have to keep on my toes.

Once, the locks were glued. Another time, the tyres were let
down. People in my hearing started talking about how someone had
had their tyres slashed and sugar put in their petrol tank which
destroys the engine. Simple intimidation, bullying.

Undaunted I tried. I knew that the whole section went drinking at
lock-ins (in pubs after hours) while they were supposed to be
patrolling. I was on my own though and every time I thought I had
them they were mysteriously tipped off. Whether it was Tommy, or
the beat bobbies I never found out but it was beginning to get me
down. I never really told Pat that I was concerned but as my Guardian
Angel would have it, we were invited to a party at my old OSD partner
Peter's, mum's house in Rainhill. We were still very friendly with
Peter and my old OSD section, we had after all been through a lot
together.

As the party went on I was button holed by Dickie who asked me
how things were going. I had had a few drinks by then and poured out
my troubles and fears. It turned out that Dick had been at Eaton road
a few years before and was reputedly one of the worst of the bunch
then. A hard man and a hard drinker. His wife had died of cancer and
he had found his God, become tea-total and cleaned up his act turning
his back on his old ways. He had then ended up in the OSD with his
new clean image but Dick still had his dark side as we the unit knew.

Dick listened quietly and told me who the culprits were before I
told him. *How did you know*', I said.

*'I used to be one of them he said. Leave it with me, and don't worry any more. Now what are you drinking, mine is an orange juice.'*

Well when I returned to work the following week, I was approached by the section who thus far had made my life a misery. I was amazed and asked the ring leader what was going on.

*'Well Dick says you are sound, sarge. He made us an offer we couldn't refuse. You'll have no more problems here.'*

And so that was it. No more problems, arrest rates up. No issues, no drinking as far as I could tell and a pat on the back from the Divisional Commander for our good work.

By the end of the year I was invited to Dick's promotion do to Inspector and invited back to the OSD as a Sergeant.

**RESULT**

# Treat Those Two Imposters Just the Same

> '**The more that you read, the more things you will know, the more that you learn, the more places you'll go.**'
> (Dr Seuss)

 In the last chapter I related my time in the Eaton Road Day and EP section and how by the second half of 1983 having successfully sorted out my section at Huyton and then those at Eaton Road, with the help of a couple of key fellow travellers, I was invited back to the OSD as a Sergeant.

I left 'D' Divison and 'Ann-Ann' in September 1983. I had been away from the OSD for two years and had learnt a great deal about surviving as a supervisor in that time. I was very flattered to be invited back so quickly to my spiritual home; the job I loved and understood. Reputation largely intact if not enhanced in terms of my abilities to sort out problem children.

The OSD hierarchy had changed significantly since I had been gone. A Chief Superintendent was now in charge and the OSD had been expanded to include the Dog and Mounted Sections. Peter Smith, the Chief Inspector who had been the beating heart of the team had gone to pastures new and impending retirement. There were a new set of Inspectors too, Eric had been promoted as had my old Inspector Gerry and I was with an unknown Inspector, Paul and given my own Unit of crazies.

Paul was an active leader, a risk taker on the cusp of recklessness but with a total inability to attend to administration in any form which he delegated to his sergeants including me. More good experience in hindsight but a pain at the time. All he wanted to do was get out and arrest people which really wasn't the job of the Inspector.

My Unit were indeed crazies. Ray, was an ex military Policeman without conscience or soul from a criminal family on St Johns estate (my old beat). He had escaped them in the army and had arrested several of his own family since without demur. He was however good to have at your back and 100% solid if prone to casual violence. Ray left the Police in 1985 and became a pub landlord in central Manchester.

Ian we called the Honey Monster after the Sugar Puffs Creature. He was 6 feet 4 inches and heavy set with it. He was even more prone to casual violence though intelligent enough to have aspirations. He did not however have a conscience. He too was from Huyton Quarry. He had a tiny fat wife who was an insurance clerk and bullied him as Trefor's wife had, him. Ian eventually became a Chief Inspector, long before me in fact but was sucked into organised crime in the mid 1990's and, convicted of data theft offences, he went to prison.

Ronnie was an enigma. He was intelligent and well-read with a fine vocabulary and great general knowledge. Married to Beryl who was a policewoman and a bit masculine, Ron collected poo, from different animals and displayed it in a cabinet. He was very odd but mild mannered and very polite with quite a social conscience and tended to stick up for the under dog. Again however, with little provocation he was prone to casual violence. Ron ended up with the Force Helicopter Team and served to an honourable retirement.

John was a clown and, though a good locker-up and very loyal was bullied by the others and a as a result wanted to be liked by them and was thus easily led. He ended up as a Detective Superintendent.

Tony the last member of the Unit was a thin intense guy from Southport. When I arrived he was unhappy and never really got on with the others and in return they didn't trust him. Although he stayed on while I was there he left very shortly after I did. He retired as a Sergeant.

As you can see then I was more of a zoo keeper at first. Nonetheless within a few months I had them more or less under control and fiercely loyal to me which turned them from a potential liability into a sound Unit.

I arrived as I said in late September and from the off it was busy and pretty intense. In late October of 1983 a murder occurred in the Wirral, actually in Cheshire but that force had no major incident capacity so we were loaned to them to undertake the murder enquiry. I was required to set up the murder control and run the house to house enquiries. This experience served me well many years later when I became an evaluator but more of that later.

After three weeks in Burton village Hall, and my crazies docilely undertaking House to House, public disorder exploded across the country and our focus suddenly changed completely.

The 1980s was a difficult time for much of working Britain, and policing picket lines at the resultant strikes kept me busy for the next couple of years.  I got a new driveway with the overtime – but I certainly earned that money.

When Margaret Thatcher came to power in 1980 following the Industrial anarchy of the late 1970s she enacted radical industrial relations legislation which curbed the power of Unions and Workers.

In November 1983 there was a serious test of this legislation when the owner of the Stockport Messenger newspaper, Eddie Shah dismissed some strikers. Printing Unions organised a massive turnout of pickets at Shah's works in Warrington.  Once again we in the OSD were deployed to assist Cheshire, to police the resulting major disorder.

*'I want you to draw your batons and charge'*

177

This was Inspector 'Crazy Horse' who had been placed in charge of our OSD Group while our own Inspector Paul continued with the Burton murder enquiry. I was possibly the youngest sergeant there. We were among hundreds of officers as a tense situation began escalating into violence. We complied and the group we targeted retreated along the road before us, halting beyond our reach whenever we stopped.

*'Come-on; and again'* (not called Crazy Horse for nothing)

So we went again, and again. After four charges of twenty or so yards we were now some distance from our own lines who were busy holding back the crowds and I could see those in front of us circling on the edge of the floodlights to both sides. There was a genuine danger we half dozen would be surrounded, and then what.

*'I don't think we should go any further Boss?'* I challenged.

As the son of a Ford factory worker and trades union shop steward, I had some sympathy with the hundreds of mostly middle-

aged workers just like my dad shouting at anyone who tried to cross their picket line (although with hindsight there were a good few 'rent-a-mob' young student Trots who wouldn't recognise a working man if they fell over him, stirring the pot).

*'Because they are all rioting scum bags!'*

*'But they're decent people, Sir, I think we should stop and get back to the others.'*

*'You refusing me?, Its an ORDER Sergeant Gill,'*

*'Yes, Sir, I am. We're going back to our line. I would suggest you come with us'.*

My men followed me without argument and even Ray who instinctively obeyed a command agreed with me. I didn't like refusing an order and knew there would be repercussions' Crazy Horse' was not a man to cross, yet I knew that the inspector had lost the plot. His Action Man tactics could have led to fighting, injuries, even a fatality.

It's possible that, with hindsight, he agreed: my refusal was never brought up again, though our relationship was scratchy ever after and Peter Smith who had been brought back to command us as his Swan-Song later told me I had done the right thing.

The incident though had the incidental effect of showing my own expectations and started to establish my Unit's own shared boundaries of behaviour.

Maybe I was going soft, or maybe I sympathised with the strikers and pickets at the time because my own father could indeed have been there, but on the second night as we travelled back to Liverpool on the Force Coach along the M62 we came across a small convoy of pickets who had been stopped. I was sat at the front and recognised a gobby bloke being roughly handled as Kenny, Pat's cousin's husband who I knew was a printer.

I never really liked Kenny, a typical Scouse Jack-the-lad (he now runs a girly bar in Thailand). Nonetheless my latent altruism took over. I got off the coach and took Kenny to one side. He was both shocked and relieved to see me I think. Anyway, I saved him, saw him on his way and told the bobbies who had stopped him to leave him be. My good deed for the day.

I did a similar deed a couple of weeks later when we were brought in to assist with a raid on a pub in Netherton which is near Maghull where we lived following a large disturbance. I recognised my cousin who I hadn't seen for years who was not involved but could well have been inadvertently arrested unfairly and managed to usher him out and send hm on his way unharmed.

Was this the type of behaviour I railed against when I was a young bobby at Huyton or was it different. I don't know, but I do know that this more mature and experienced version of myself was more inclined to give people the benefit of the doubt than I had been in my youth.

Just a few days after Christmas, Pat went into Fazakerley Hospital to have Vicky; our third. It wasn't a straightforward birth and when she was delivered we could see that she had been in distress in the womb but in the end both turned out to be OK. She came on 29th December and the following day I was back at work.

I am very superstitious about New Years's eve. I believe that what you do at the stroke of midnight at New Year will in some way reflect your fate in the year to come. We always try to be together at New Year. I always volunteered to work over Christmas and have New Years Eve off and even on the one occasion I had to work it, when I worked with Mike in the OSD in 1980, we had managed to be with our families at midnight, me in Mrs McLoughlin's house and Mike a few houses away at his mother's, police car parked outside, before we resumed patrol at 1 am.

In 1983 though, Pat and I couldn't be together. Pat tells me she cried in hospital with baby Vicky listening to the ship's horns on the Mersey at midnight while I was elsewhere. In fact elsewhere at the stroke of midnight was the Holt Pub in Kensington near Old Swan where we were clearing out a pub, then fighting with people on the pavement outside for the next thirty or so minutes. Maybe that's why 1984 was such a violent and bad year for me personally.

There was a bit of a lull in major incidents in the first couple of months of 1984 but we were put on high alert for a possible international crisis leading to a nuclear conflict following an incident called the "Able Archer War Scare". This had occurred over a ten day period in the November of 1983, when a NATO exercise went wrong and caused the Soviet Union to go on the highest level of nuclear readiness. We in the OSD were briefed on evacuation plans and there was a high level of tension and worry. In fact my madmen and I made our own contingency arrangements that in the event of the balloon going up we would arm ourselves from the St Anne Street armoury, collect our families and find ourselves a safe haven. Deluded maybe but so much was the degree of concern, unbeknown to the public.

In March of 1984 the miners' strike began. We in the OSD were kept back within Merseyside as the Force's strategic reserve while the Divisions were sent to other forces to assist. We only had two Collieries, both in St Helens and so were used to Police these. It meant we got little overtime but all the hassle of the interventions.

Pat and I had moved to Maghull in the autumn of 1982 but as we were still very familiar with St Helens we attended the St Helens Show in the summer of 1984. We had the kids with us but it didn't stop me getting some verbal abuse from still striking miners who recognised me from the picket lines nearby, much to the embarrassment and concern of Pat, though we were safe enough. Few would consciously get on the wrong side of the OSD in those days.

When you read about what are the most common things that cause acute stress the list is pretty consistent. Major life events, death marriage, children, new job, moving house. Well in 1983 and 1984 I had the lot and I was probably as close as I have ever come to breaking down though I was not conscious of it while it was happening.

We had moved to an older, bigger house in the autumn of 1982 so when I moved jobs a year later things were still pretty difficult and expensive with a lot of work to do and not much money to do it with. I had the new job of course and was in the second year of my Open University degree with three children under five. Len was just three, Lizzy one and Vicky a new born. Into the bargain my Dad, who had been apparently hale and hearty when we moved in, sickened badly in 1983 with what we thought was his chest but turned out to be heart failure. He died in October 1984 and it affected me more that I was prepared for or even recognised at the time.

There were warning signs of my stress though. During the summer of 1984 my Unit were deployed on evenings to the Wirral and I had chest Pain. I was only twenty eight but I told the lads to take me into A&E for a check. It turned out I was OK and the hospital told me it was anxiety but it did worry me.

A couple of months later we were all in Crown Court and walking back to St Anne Street through an underpass. I was suddenly unable to get up the slope. The others helped me and got me back to the station and it turned out I had a bad case of pneumonia and I was off work for a week. Clearly my health was being undermined by stress I can see that now.

But it wasn't just my health that was affected. As my dad got worse in the late summer of 1984 he was in and out of hospital and I got him a recliner chair when he was home, he could scarcely breath and in behaviour unlike him I could see panic in his eyes sometimes when he was in distress.

I think the strain affected my judgement too. I would phone home or the hospital and have quite long conversations about how dad was doing and for privacy I took to using the phone in the doctor's room in stations I was visiting. Well in the end it was my undoing. Classed as unauthorised use I was in breach of the high ethical standards required in the OSD and sent back to Division. In fairness I wasn't disciplined and nothing ever appeared on my personal file but I think the bosses recognised my judgement was off and maybe I was becoming unreliable.

They looked after me though. I was sent to Tuebrook Police Station. My Inspector was none other than my old OSD Sergeant Dickie and the new Superintendent Pat Carragher. Nowadays a more famous scion of the Carragher family is the footballer and commentator Jamie Carragher but in my day his uncle Pat was by far more important and famous or infamous depending on your point of view. Pat Carragher had taken over from Peter Smith as Chief Inspector OSD and was feared, even hated by many for his cold ruthlessness. I was fortunate that he liked me because I was straight and a hard worker and thief-taker. He was the one that made the decision that I couldn't continue given the pressures on me but made sure I went with him as he was promoted to be Superintendent at Tuebrook. Between them Pat and Dick took a lot of pressure off me and allowed me to get back on my feet after Dad died in mid October.

I was posted as the Tuebrook Bridewell Sergeant and my assistant which we called the Bridewell Patrol or BP was a lovely policewoman called Jane who was married to a Dog Handler and had

185

more or less the same service as I did. She was also a friend of my old
partner Peter, so I was surrounded by people who were supportive
and valued me. As the Bridewell Sergeant I was responsible for
maintaining the Station and looking after any prisoners brought in.

It was actually a good time to take up the job because the Police
and Criminal Evidence Act (PACE) was introduced as a pilot in
Merseyside just weeks after I started in post which meant that within
months I was one of only a handful of Sergeants in the country
conversant with the new law which would soon change the culture of
Police prisoner management forever. It put me in an excellent
'expert' position and improved both my profile and reputation. It
seems that it is not just in literature and on film that when one door
closes, another opens.

Meanwhile though, the Miners dispute continued and in my new
station I was no longer constrained to be one of the strategic reserve
so I was able to volunteer for mutual aid to other forces and make
some extra money. I went as part of a Police Support Unit (PSU) to
Nottinghamshire, Northumberland and Durham, where there were
more picket lines than the home police forces could deal with on their

own. I'd work a 15-hour day, then at night sleep on a put-up bed at a military camp requisitioned for the purpose. Always, you had to be on your guard. Journalists as well as strikers would look for your weak spot. One indisciplined comment, one uncontrolled gesture could lead to a newspaper photo, a headline made and disciplinary action.

The PSU to Durham was the most enjoyable I think. For a start we were housed at the Durham Police Training Centre which was unoccupied at the time, and a good job it was, otherwise the recruits would have got a very jaundiced view of their more experienced colleagues. Our PSU consisted of an Inspector, two Sergeants (Bob and myself) and twenty men (women were not allowed on PSUs and I believe that should still be the case though this view may not now be fashionable).

The Inspector was known as Biffo. Now it is, I know, common for Biff to be an acronym for something rude but in Biffo's case this wasn't true. He was simply called Biffo because he bore a remarkable likeness to the cartoon character of the same name in the Beano.

Biffo was almost at the end of his service and his day job was literally a day job, he was the Admin Inspector in D Division and was on the PSU under considerable sufferance. He lived in Runcorn and regaled us with very credible stories of the ghost who haunted his house. Most of the time though he was asleep or drunk.

We were in Durham to police the colliery at Tursdale (which we inevitably called Turds Dale) a few miles from the city. We got up at 4am and were outside the Colliery entrance by 5am ready to receive the 'scabs' bus and have our daily tussle with the pickets. We had finished by 7am and had a similar tussle as the afternoon shift came in at 1pm. The rest of our day and evening was our own.

Bob was tea-total as was I so we tended to use our off duty time in the early evening to have a look around the sights of Durham and retire to our beds in our shared room by 10pm, very boring. Our section however were not so moderate in their habits and with an average age of about twenty two and an average mental age of about seven few turned into their beds more than an hour before they were due to get up the next morning having had a full nights drinking and womanising. The main game seemed to be the collection of women's underwear I seem to remember.

Bob and I were required to drag (literally in some cases) the miscreants from their beds and help to dress those few who had bothered to undress before collapsing into their pits, hand them a paper bag containing a packed lunch, drink carton and straw and bully them into the two personnel carriers we crammed ourselves into.

Biffo was far too old for womanising but he did like a drink. Bob or I would toss a coin and the loser would be obliged to get the

Inspector out of his bed, put his uniform trousers and jacket over his pyjamas and half carry him to one of the Carriers where he would be jammed in the front seat between the driver and his dresser of the day, to snore and fart his way through the high jinx of the morning session.

By the afternoon he was fine and remembered little of the morning. We were fortunate that Turds Dale provided relatively little trouble for us to deal with and we were able to keep Biffo and our band of heroes out of the way of anyone more senior for the weeks we were there.

The Nottinghamshire trips were more demanding. We were camped out in a large aircraft hangar on the Bawtry RAF base with about 400 camp beds set out in rows inside. We deployed to several collieries as far as Retford. I thought we were pretty effective in dealing with public order and were always put in the thick of the action. At the time we took it as a compliment but now I wonder was it because we were expendable.

Our general standard of discipline and dress was poor if not disgraceful and compared to PSUs from county forces such as

Lancashire we must have looked like a penal battalion. One day we were parked up at a colliery and the Lancashire contingent I think it was, and a Yorkshire group were deployed to keep the pickets away from the strikers. There was a degree of 'argy-bargy' but not that much. All of a sudden a few car loads of flying pickets arrived and the picket line swelled and became significantly more animated and rowdy.

*'Ok Merseyside, out the vans and over to the picket line'*

The order was relayed from the incident commander and we were turfed out of our steamy fug into the cold morning air. As we tumbled out the Lancashire PSU stood down and marched smartly past us,

*'Left, right, left, right, left, right'*

No such behaviour from my dishevelled smelly bunch so I shouted ironically.

*'Merseyside PSU, prepare to shamble, SHAMBLE,'*

Taking up our position we dealt with the threat, dragged a few miscreants away and shut them down. Once the workers' bus had passed, the sound level subsided and the flying pickets began to leave we heard, *'Merseyside stand down, back to your vehicles'*, and as we shambled back to our carriers we saw that Lancashire was back, *'Left right, left right, left right. HALT'*

We returned to our billet only to find that our kit had been rifled and a lot of equipment had been stolen. The only clue to the culprits were printed calling cards scattered across our beds carrying the legend,

## 'I'VE MET THE MET

But back in Tuebrook, once I got my head around PACE one day was like the next.

Arrive fifteen minutes before handover.

Check the prisoners, sign the sheets, check the safe, sign the sheet, check the radios, sign the sheet, check the memo book, sign the book. Sign Jane's pocket book. Fill in my own pocket book, on duty, refreshments, off duty.

*'Sarge, I'm going for a Kebab on Smithdown, do you want one?'*

Bell rings, check the prisoners, sign the sheet.

Bell rings, new prisoner, get the circumstances, book the prisoner in, put them in a cell, sign the sheet.

Bell rings, caller at the desk,

*'Sarge, he wants to speak to you'*, says Jane, sign the sheet.

*'Sarge, I'm going for a Wispa, from the garage do you want one?'*

So it went on, and on and on.

The wee small hours dragged, I spent more time with Jane than I did with Pat and watched over the months as her marriage imperceptibly broke down and her husband ran off with another Policewoman.

I became the confidante and councillor for others on the shift too as I was always there as an ear, not going anywhere.

My first escape attempt was in late 1984. I noticed a small advert in a daily newspaper. A recruitment drive was underway for Police Officers of Sergeant rank to join the Royal Papua New Guinea (PNG) Police in the rank of Inspector. I didn't actually know where PNG was so I got as many books out of the library as possible. I studied both of them! Which told me that it was near Australia, primitive, tribal and the people were in places still cannibals I applied and Pat reluctantly agreed.

In the late 1970s the British Empire was in its last throes. There were a few overseas opportunities that still popped up for international policing in the old colonial model though. Bermuda was the most desirable though it was only for single men so that was out for me, though a few blokes from Huyton went out and had a great time.

The other plum was Hong Kong. This was accompanied but generally they wanted experienced Sergeants and Inspectors and by the time I had enough experience they had stopped recruiting. So I thought I would give PNG a whirl.

I passed the paper sift and went for interview in London and actually got the job. We would need to put the kids in boarding school in Darwin from aged 7 but that didn't apply yet. We would live in a colonial villa and I would be the chief of police and magistrate

193

at my posting which was initially for five years. All very exciting. I got my posting to the North Solomon Islands and was about to resign from Merseyside and had actually notified a removals firm to start shipping my stuff and put my house up for sale when there was some sort of coup d'etat and the job was withdrawn after a decision to indigenise the police and throw all the whites out.

I later discovered I had had a very lucky escape. The posting in the Solomons was in a place called Bougainville and in 1988 a vicious little civil war began. The conflict was the largest conflict in Oceania since the end of World War Two, with an estimated 15,000–20,000 Bougainvilleans dead.

If I had gone, then I would have found myself, and the family in the middle of it!

I did eventually meet another colleague from North Yorkshire who had also been accepted but he had had the misfortune of being quicker than me and had actually resigned, sold his house and shipped his furniture days before the process was cancelled. He ended up losing his rank on re-joining and never did see his furniture again.

### Then one night

*'Sarge have you seen this weeks orders?'* Says Jane

*'They're looking for first aid trainers, there's a course, might be a little break away from the monotony.'*

So I applied, and got it, because no-one else applied.

194

*'You seem to have an aptitude for this,,'* the Instructor told me. *'Have you thought of applying for an instructor's course?'*

*'Not really',* I still wanted to be an action man.

I applied. I was selected to go on an Instructor's course in Harrogate. Two weeks before I went though I was told that the course was changing, did I still want to go?

Police training was in the process of a shake-up. The move was towards adult education, student-centred learning and now being called the 'Trainer's Course'. The change sat well with me although I had no real idea what to expect. I had just finished my degree in my own time to boot!

So in September 1986 almost two years to the day since I arrived at Tuebrook off I went to Yorkshire and a twelve week residential course at the Home Office Central Planning Unit which over the next decade would become a very familiar and special place to me.

Twelve of us, all Sergeants (except one) from forces across the North of England attended the first Trainers Course. We overlapped with the last Instructor's course who were being trained to deliver lectures and still had a heavy emphasis on traditional teaching methods and marching in the military style. We would have a very different experience with emphasis on psychology, reflection, varied teaching methods and novel approaches to discipline and coaching.

The Instructors course were understandably annoyed seeing their course as obsolete before they had even finished it. We of course wound them up unmercifully and managed to convince them,

195

in the crucible of a long residential environment that we were being trained as some sort of Jedi, learning such things as telepathy, mind reading and levitation. Dressing up in the evening in long saffron robes and chanting buddhist like. Sounds stupid I know but we actually got them to believe it, and so a legend was born!

We were of course being trained as the vanguard of an entire culture change, as change agents though we had never heard the term before we were trained to provoke, and to undermine the existing system. After ten weeks we were sent out to undertake 'Teaching Practice' at the various district training centres across the North. I went back to Bruche where I trained in 1976. The place had not changed at all and was effectively in aspic.

The big blonde lad in the back row (photo below) was from Lancashire and played Rugby for the British Police. He ended up actually fighting with a member of the centre's permanent staff, another equally belligerent Sergeant from South Yorkshire.

I was dragged before the centre's senior officer known as the Commandant who accused me of dressing inappropriately. In truth I wore the best clothes I could afford at the time with three under fives and a fourth on the way. Egged on by the staff from the CPU I took no prisoners and in the privacy of his office I told him to stuff it, confident in the support I was promised (and got) from the CPU. I gained few friends among the staff or management at Bruche but fortunately had no wish to work there.

All in all the course was a good one, I learnt to be a very good Trainer and it has served me well ever since. I doubt I would have achieved the things I did without the course. In truth the Police Trainers Course (version 1) put us many years ahead of teachers in other public services but at what cost?

Those teaching us were themselves novices in the educational use of psychological techniques, what is called Rogerian Counselling and generally messing with people's heads. I was fine, I have robust mental strength and I had a stable supportive family to keep me grounded. Others were not so lucky. More than 15% of those attending the Trainers course in the first two years of its introduction suffered metal breakdown and were unable to cope with the methods used to mould them into the new culture. This led some to marital breakdown and deprived the British Police of some good people who might have thrived in other circumstances. In hindsight this was an unacceptable price to pay for change.

# We Are Family

> **'Raising children is, in a sense, the reason the
> society exists in the first place.
> It's the most important thing that happens.'**
> (Michael Crichton – The Lost World)

Len Gill with his wife Pat and children Leonard, Elizabeth, Victoria and Sarah. MB 102.

The day after I became a father, I was at the Billinge Hospital registrar office at 9 a.m.

I was so thrilled to have a son that I wanted to be there the moment the official's office opened, ready to register his birth.

*'His name is Leonard,'* I told the registrar. *'He was born on 15th April 1980.'*

Pat, who'd had a difficult forceps birth, was still on the ward upstairs in the main building of the hospital– which was just as well, really, because she wanted our firstborn to be called James, after her own father!

I'll admit, she wasn't impressed when I told her what I'd done. But she got over it. And of course, years later, we did go on to have Edward James our sixth, last but by no means least, who carries the names of both his grandfathers– so Pat's father's name did get to live on within the family after all in the end.

Pat became pregnant with Lenny in the summer of 1979, probably as a result of the corn dollies in the west country villages we stayed in on our belated honeymoon aboard our 2CV chariot. She was working in Billinge hospital as a pupil midwife throughout the pregnancy and, by the time of her finals, her pregnancy was quite advanced. So much so that she was admitted with some pregnancy related complications and had to be wheeled into the exam room drugged to the eyeballs and heavily pregnant. She failed the exam of course and it isn't surprising as she can remember nothing. In her appeal though she was forced to sit a Viva Voce where she was asked questions live by a panel of doctors and midwives. She passed with

201

flying colours but it was to no avail and neither of us were keen for her to continue and re-sit the year so she became a full time mum.

She was overdue in the end and the day before, in an effort to get things going we spent the day walking around the Ideal Home exhibition at Aintree Race Course. It did the trick and she went in. I was however in the OSD and doing security on the Jimmy Kelly Trial in St Helens.

Kelly was a drunk from Huyton who had died whilst being arrested in Huyton by officers from my old shift as it turned out. All the officers involved were subsequently charged with murder but before this an inquest was held and my Unit was assigned to maintain 24 hour security at the coroner's court.

# Jimmy Kelly: '36 bruises on body'

While mystery still surrounds the findings of an official post mortem into the death of Huyton labourer Mr. James Kelly, it has been revealed that multiple injuries were a contributory factor to his death while in police custody last June.

The Kelly family claimed to-day that the report by Dr. John Torry, the pathologist called in by them, concluded that multiple injuries and alcoholic intoxication were contributory factors to death.

The report showed that Mr. Kelly, 55, a bachelor, of Sleaford Road, had 36 bruises on his body, a shattered jawbone and crushed vertebrae.

Top level talks were held between Dr. Torry, Home Office pathologist Dr. John Benstead and Professor Alan Usher, head of forensic science at Sheffield University, on August 19. Professor Usher, called in by Merseyside's Chief Constable, has not yet issued his findings.

It will be his report that will be forwarded to the Director of Public Prosecutions for consideration.

Dr. Torry reveals in his report that several weeks prior to Mr. Kelly's death on June 21, he attended Broadgreen Hospital where doctors diagnosed angina.

There is no doubt, in Dr. Torry's opinion, that Mr. Kelly died from unnatural causes.

Mr. Kelly had been out celebrating the return of his brother from Australia the night he died. He was arrested on waste ground in Barkbeth Road, taken to Huyton Police Station. A few hours later was found to be dead on arrival at Whiston Hospital.

A West Midlands police chief is investigating the allegations at Huyton and another claim at nearby Kirkby.

As an aside, one of those officers charged but subsequently cleared was called Fred. He was married to Elaine, you will remember her as the Prescot driver who helped me deal with the Rose and Crown Irishman.

Anyway, Fred's nickname was 'The Viking'. He was a small thin even wizened man who had been an RAF Police dog handler and quite ugly. Not the picture you may have formed of a bearded blonde Thor lookalike. He worked at Huyton for a bit but also did a turn in the dog section (RAF you see!) and at Kirkby later in his service. I tell you this to explain his moniker.

Fred was actually called the Viking because he is to my knowledge the only policeman to have been charged with, appeared before court, and subsequently acquitted of Murder (Jimmy Kelly), Rape (refusing to pay a prostitute in the rear of the dog van allegedly) and Pillage (for that of course read Theft), when money went missing from the safe he was responsible for as a Bridewell Patrol.

Fred was an unpleasant man but managed to survive and retire with a full pension and unbelievably a long service and good conduct medal. How such a lovely girl as Elaine married and stayed with him till she died tragically young of cancer, I will never know, but she did; and Fred the Viking remains a good story.

Anyway back to Lenny. When I got the call that Pat was in labour I was driven straight to the hospital in our personnel carrier in full uniform (my car was later dropped off by a colleague which is how I got home), was taken to the delivery room where I donned a plastic oversuit.

I was roasting. It was a difficult birth and I was ushered out at the denouement when forceps were needed. Len came out as a result with a pointy bruised head like an alien. Pat looked like death, but I loved them both and was so proud.

Lenny was the apple of our eye and the centre of our lives. We lived, us three and the dogs, in Truro Close which had no heating and was so cold the net curtains froze to the inside of the windows in the

winter of 1980 and Mr McLoughlin gave us an electric Dimplex heater
so we didn't get hypothermia but we could barely afford to use
because electricity was so expensive. We all slept together to keep
warm despite this. It cost a fortune to run back in the days of 18.5%
mortgage rates and crazy inflation of 18%.

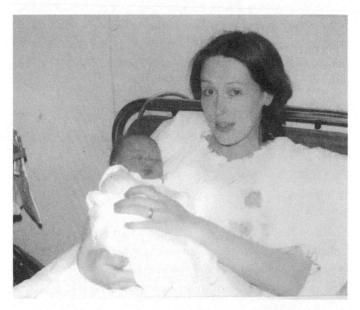

When he began to walk in the May of 1981, we went on holiday to
Crete and stayed in a small villa. I have been a member of the IPA the
International Police Association, a police friendship organisation
since I joined and the trip to Crete was an ideal chance I thought to
use its advantages. I wrote away and received a letter back from
Greece telling me to call at the local Police Station on arrival and they
would help me if I needed anything. The contact's name was Christa.

On arrival Pat, I and the baby in a pram went to the station in Agios Nikolaos which was then a small fishing village, beginning its expansion. Pat and the baby waited outside and I went in to be greeted by a young very attractive policewoman who told me she was 'at my disposal' and had arranged to move out of her barracks and stay at my villa with me. She was somewhat crestfallen when I introduced her to Pat and the baby but nonetheless provided assistance to hire a car for free and provided an emergency contact if I had any trouble.

Our only luxury in St Helens was a rented TV and Betamax video recorder which was a better type than the VHS which nonetheless eventually dominated the market. Together we had a cold but idyllic family life until the riots hit in the July which I have already related at length. Pat and Lenny relocated to Pat's mums for the duration and by the time things had settled down and I was promoted Pat was pregnant again.

The winter of 1981 was bitterly cold. We thought we had been cold the previous year but it was nothing compared to 1981. I stupidly failed to park the car in the garage at the start of winter and as a result I couldn't start it and it never moved for nearly two months, snow and ice bound. I was reduced to going to work on my motorbike, (a Honda 400/4), by this time though it was a deadly exercise and I came off in the ice more than once. Pregnant Pat was reduced to sliding gingerly up the hill to the shops with the baby in a pram while I was at work and in the depths of the snow, ice and fog she came back one day to find we had been burgled.

The woman next door, Jackie was, according to her, a clerk of some kind but we suspected she supplemented her income in other ways and had a constant stream of boyfriends and male visitors. One of these was a gypsy looking type who was altogether too gregarious. Pat returned home that day and the house was even colder than normal. Bonnie was nowhere to be seen and she found the dog locked in the under stairs 'Harry Potter' cupboard. Sophie of course was off fighting crime at this point.

The large picture window in the living room was smashed and our Video Recorder gone. The Police were called and a dog handler appeared and tracked a scent to next door but with no more to go on the burglary remained unsolved and our gypsy thief disappeared forever along with our video recorder.

Pat was never the same in that house. She wanted to move and was frightened to be alone. I fitted an alarm system and a panic button but all to no avail and we put the house up for sale but it wouldn't sell. Eventually I agreed to part exchange it for an older house with the Barratt house builder and we got ready to move to Maghull in North Liverpool but it took a while as repairs were needed before we could go.

Meanwhile our Elizabeth Alexandra, my second child was born in May of 1982 also in Billinge Hospital. She came right in the middle of the Falklands conflict and to add to Pat's anxiety she convinced herself I was going to get conscripted and go to war, despite my reassurances. Elizabeth was awkward right from the off. She lay in the wrong position consistently and had to be turned regularly by the midwife risking bleeding. Nonetheless when she came out it was an easier birth than Lenny and she was beautiful with a great tan, which turned out to be jaundice due to awkwardness no doubt and spent her early days in an incubator.

Lizzy had barely arrived , she was ten weeks old and we moved. To make matters worse I was in the first year of my Open University degree and had to attend summer school, a residential week in Bath. We moved in and the very next day I went to Bath.

Our new house, in Rosslyn Avenue Maghull was much bigger. A 1930s semi with a huge linear garden was a delight though my dad, (still well then) and I, shifted twenty tons of soil in wheel barrows to sort out the garden and begin the job of landscaping. This was of course the time I was struggling with the Day and EP problems so I was being pulled both ways and I was forced to do lots of overtime

which was good for the finances, (the mortgage was rather large), but
difficult for Pat with a new baby and a toddler.

By the summer of 1983 though, things were easier. I had sorted
out work, with Dickie help and we were more comfortable in the
house. At least the garden looked a bit better and we had done the

initial decorating though there was still a lot to do. It was at this point Pat announced she was once more pregnant, betrayed by the fact that Lizzy no longer wanted to breast feed. Vicky, (Victoria Rebecca named after a character in Duncton Wood, a book Pat was reading during that pregnancy) was born in December 1983 in Fazackerley Hospital in Liverpool and I have already related her arrival.

Over the next couple of years we were very family oriented. The only people we socialised with were my OSD pal Peter and his wife Nicki, an American who now lived over here. They too had a large young family, Nicki had three children from her previous marriage and they had a baby, Jenny, of their own so we had a lot in common. We had very little money to spare but did our best to get the kids away on breaks, staying in youth hostels and cramming into the car with the seats down and bin bags full of clothes and sleeping bags around them for safety. We went first to Pembrokeshire staying at the youth Hostel in St Davids, then we went to stay in the Youth Hostel at Hindhead in the Devil's Punchbowl Surrey where, in an effort to push the car out of a ditch Pat did her back in and was laid up for a while. She never really fixed the problem and has a bad back even now.

Finally we had a holiday with Hoseasons, taking a small chalet in the Norfolk Broads to celebrate Lizzie's birthday (the birthday party we held in a recently opened McDonalds).

We spent the days on the waterways aboard the included small motor launch, the kids each taking turns at helping me steer.

In the spring of 1986 there was yet another on the way. By the time I attended the Trainers course in Harrogate Pat was six months pregnant with Sarah and we spent a lovely weekend in Harrogate visiting the sights and we had a lovely day at the Harewood House Estate. Sarah Patricia after Mrs Miller my grandmother and Pat's mum was born on 3rd January 1987 once more in Fazackerley and then it was to be a temporary hiatus to our family while I established myself with a change of direction in work in a training role and concentrated on finishing my OU Degree as quickly as I could doing two modules per year instead of the usual one.

Pat and I always wanted a large family. Close friendships haven't been a thing in either of our lives – family is what counts.

We had no idea what was ahead and saw ourselves staying in the suburban environment, little knowing that our young family, and two

more, Katharine Beatrice and Edward James would come along
before too long and soon we would all end up living the country life.

# Out of the Frying Pan

**'Take the straight and narrow path**
**And if you start to slide,**
**Give a little whistle!**
**Give a little whistle!**
**And always let your conscience be your guide!'**

(Pinocchio – Walt Disney, 1940)

*'Where's Steve,' I said as I entered the administration Unit in Tuebrook, I was supposed to meet him here at two,'* the Admin Inspector was sniggering and looking out the window overlooking Newsham Park.

*'Oh he's outside Sarge, He's on Helicopter duty.'* Said the day duties constable.

*'What',* I said, looking out the window now myself competing with five other rubber-neckers, *'Whose that down there you're looking at,'*

*'That's him Sarge, in the fluorescent jacket,'*

214

**The Flying Squad?**

ALTHOUGH Tuesday dawned damp and gloomy on the outskirts of Liverpool it was to be a special day: David Steel, the Liberal leader, was arriving by helicopter on a playing field in the suburb of Tue Brook.

As is customary these days, the local C I D had the area staked out in advance. Alliance supporters were gathered, the odd heckler lurking with them to watch the descent of the Boy David.

Just then, an apparition. Walking out proudly on to the Newsham Park recreation ground was a police officer, dressed in Day-Glo yellow, wearing goggles and carrying two red table tennis bats.

The distant throb of a helicopter rotor sounded above the murk and the policeman, pulling himself to his full height, marched with his eyes skyward to the white H on the grass. As the machine broke cloud he began to motion slowly with the bats, beckoning Steel's pilot to *terra firma.*

At this point the C I D men, who had been watching with astonishment from the outfield, ran in towards the officer and apprehended him. Under questioning it emerged that he had joined Tue Brook police station nearby as a rookie constable just days before and was the victim of a practical joke.

He told his new colleagues: "This was my first big assignment."

*'What the F**** is going on Peter,'* I address the Admin Inspector now, a man of normally impeccable correctness presently red in the face and guffawing. *'It was just too tempting, Lenny, that boy is an idiot, We've sent him out on Helicopter duty, it's a wind up, he'll twig in a minute.'*

In the distance my poor probationer is running full tilt across the park. It is the hottest day so far of a very hot summer and he is dressed in his tunic, a plastic padded functional jacket and a further fluorescent jacket over that. Wearing his helmet tied on and a pair of plastic riot goggles he carries what appear to be paddles in each hand.'

*'You set of B*****,'* I say, *'I'm going after him to bring him in,',*

215

*'Well good luck with that see you later.'* Is the reply

I intercept Steve in the clearing of the park. He is gazing up to the sky, goggles now fixed on his eyes; waiting.

Around the clearing are groups of onlookers bemused at the sight. They were just waiting for the arrival of their MP by helicopter before this new cabaret act arrived and steals the show.

*'Steve,'* I shout from my car, *'Steve,'*

*'Hello Sarge, what's up,'*

*'Come in the car Steve, I want to speak to you,'*

*'I can't I'm on Helicopter duty,'*

*'No Steve, come here, quick, its a wind up,'*

Crestfallen he pours himself into my car and I drive away quickly, embarrassed myself.

Steve weeps in shame.

I was actually told before I finished the course that I would not be returning to Tuebrook and had been moved to be the Divisional Training Officer at Wavertree, which did cover Tuebrook, Eaton Road and Huyton so I was still on 'home turf'.

It was a great job. I had my own office, though Wavertree was a dark and dismal place designed with little natural light. The job was a uniform post which I have always preferred not least because it works out a lot cheaper than buying your own clothes for work and finally, best of all it had a car allowance. That meant I couldn't use the police cars but I could use my own car to travel around and claim the mileage which turned a not inconsiderable profit, and they gave me an interest free loan which I used to buy a nice second hand Vauxhall Cavalier. I kept that car for several years, it was fast off the mark (no dead spot like the olde model) and versatile. The only drawback I eventually found was that it was overpowered and I ended by blowing the engine up in Kent and getting stranded (but that is another story).

The post really had little in the way of job description so I was given a free hand. I was meant to mentor and counsel the probationers in the division so had to see each one at least once a month, there were around thirty at any one time. I also had to deliver some lessons by invitation at the Force Training Centre at Mather

Avenue and had to give two lessons on the promotion course which was a part time affair people did in their own time. I was given Liquor Licensing and the Wildlife and Countryside Act. I became the force expert on both.

Most of my time though was with the probationers and though deemed rather an eccentric practice I would pick them up in my car and we would go hunting for prisoners, (I was addicted I think!).

Often, I'd be driving to the training centre and see 'something' on the way. Now, other officers might have just called it in. Not me. I continued to catch and lock people up, though I was criticised for it, and rightly in hindsight.

There were still pranks though being played on the recruits, though I did my best to protect them from it. Most memorably, once, a trainee was supplied with table tennis bats so that he could use them as air traffic control paddles to land a helicopter bringing then MP David Alton to an event. All good fun but it made The Daily Telegraph the next day. Not so good, and very cruel.

I began work as DTO in early December 1986 and eighteen months later was called to see the Chief Superintendent Training Geoff who told me that he had been approached to offer me a seconded job on the staff of the Central Planning Unit in Harrogate. Geoff had been head of CID before that. He was an old school detective but carried a veneer of landed gentry though he only lived in an Edwardian villa opposite the Hoylake golf club. He was to prove a good friend in the years to come.

I managed to earn extra money too as a First-Aid Trainer with St Johns Ambulance with the blessing of the Force and have kept my hand in, First-Aid wise, to this day.

As far as CPU was concerned. The boss, Les Poole was a Metropolitan Police Commander and a character himself. He was married to an American called Florence who was a typical East Coast Liberal and he had met her when he was doing a degree at Harvard paid for by the Met.

I was one of Les and Florence's 'creatures' in that I was a product of the first 'pure' Trainers course and had well and truly been inculcated into the new philosophy and methods of Police Training where the baby had unfortunately been thrown out with the bath water.

Whilst cultural change, driven by the aftermath of the Scarman enquiry in 1982 and followed by a university led report on Police Training called 'the Stage 2 Review', was going to happen; and being heavily pushed in government. There was massive resistance from the Police themselves, and understandably.

The Home Office, Les Poole and his backers needed people inside the organisation to assault the system and bring it crashing down to be replaced with the new. My personality was just right for that. Hence my invitation.

I joined eleven other 'Trainers' who were similarly challenging and abrasive, and inculcated into the new methodologies on a twelve week residential staff course which began as usual in the summer, this time of 1988. Successful completion of the course meant I would be expected to move to Harrogate for a secondment period of three years and financial assistance was provided to re-locate my home and family. The picture shows us together with Les and Florence in the centre and Frank who was our trainer and mentor and went on to become a friend.

The post also carried promotion to Inspector and so carried a great incentive to pass. Once again the course required us to undertake a two-week attachment to a Police Training Centre and I was sent to Ashford in Kent this time. That incidentally is where my car blew up and I ended up having to get the train home to Liverpool and go into debt to get a new engine. Our mission was to 'challenge' the management at the centre but balance this with remaining within the boundaries of acceptability. We were the Home Office's 'Taliban' after all.

At the end of the attachment I had only upset the Ashford Commandant on one issue, that of 'out of bounds' areas in the centre which seemed to have no basis in common sense, otherwise I did rather well diplomacy wise.

The same couldn't be said of some of the others. In particular a bloke called Greg who is centre second row with the red tie was a Detective Sergeant from a Welsh Force who had come to us following an extended undercover operation with the Sons of Glyndwr. Greg was great, I liked him a lot and he was very clever and good fun. However during his attachment he had a little too much to drink and ended up laying out several staff members at the centre he was at (Cwmbran). Despite the best efforts of Les Poole this was a bridge too far and he had to return to force and lost the promotion.

Other than Greg we all passed and were separated into three groups. The four more diplomatic became full time trainers at the

CPU, two others went to work in Research Posts. One bloke who was already an Inspector became a Chief Inspector and the remaining four of us, the ones who were considered most likely to shake the tree I think, became evaluators whose job it was to travel between centres and be CPU commissars determining the ideological purity of the teaching staff. We weren't well liked and revelled in our role and other's dislike.

A year after our selection a new recruit training course was designed and piloted at the former Naval Base in Shotley Ipswich. I was selected from the Evaluation team to join the U.E.A. academics to be embedded with the course.

We began by shadowing the new recruits from their swearing in. Each evaluator was responsible for ten recruits from two different forces. I was allocated South Yorkshire and Warwickshire. We should really have been non judgemental but it was hard not to continue in the guise of commissar and when I arrived at Shotley wasted no time in winding up the centre management in a number of ways which resulted after about three weeks and several warnings, being hauled before the commandant who promptly banned me from the centre and packed me back to Yorkshire.

Six hours drive later I made my weary way through the CPU gate, ready for a sleep but was summoned to see Les Poole.

*'What the F**** have you been F*** doing at Shotley then'*

*'What I thought was needed'* I said, *'challenging those things I was taught to do; like you told me Sir.'*

*'Well',* said Les, *'You better get back in your car and F*** Off back there and do your job. Tell the Commandant when you get there, It's MY F****** pilot and if he's got a problem with you then pick up the phone and consult me first.'*

So off I went back to Shotley, arriving shattered in the early hours. The following morning I delivered the message and the upshot was that I could not be removed from the centre but could not undertake any evaluation either.

At this point my experience in House to House control came to the fore and I ended up as the Evaluation control co-ordinator.

Within a fortnight I had designed an analytical system based on a major crime enquiry control and was the only one on the team who actually had the full picture of what was going on. The system was so successful that it was the key to the final report and formed the basis to design a new course for those conducting evaluations which was

223

rolled out nationally and subsequently sold commercially to a number of major retail firms in the UK.

Into the bargain, and on the back of the evaluation course I undertook an MEd degree with the University of Hull and was awarded a research fellowship.

This was quickly followed by a Master of Arts Degree with the Open University and then a Post Graduate Certificate in Adult Education.

And all because I upset the Commandant at Shotley!!

During the Staff course I was also house hunting. Most of the staff at CPU tended to live in the leafy grandeur of Harrogate, one of the most expensive places in Britain to live. This included those officers who had come from down south and who of course had a hefty deposit from selling their own houses. Most of these were older and had no children. Others, less well off but again generally with no children went to Knaresborough, only a short distance away and still relatively suburban.

I determined if I was going to live in the countryside so looked further (and slightly cheaper) afield, given I needed a bigger house for the money anyway. I settled on a tiny village called Skelton-on-Ure near Ripon and traded up to a detached but with a small (actually tiny) garden on the assumption it would be less work when I was away from home. The village was still a tied village when we arrived, just 50 or so houses and most of these were occupied by workers for the Newby Hall Estate, where Charles and Camilla went for illicit weekends occasionally or so local folklore had it. There was to my astonishment no crime in Ripon and less in Skelton. Before I bought I visited the the Police Station in Ripon and asked if I should avoid anywhere crime wise. They laughed, and laughed.

I asked in Skelton too and was introduced to Terry, the gamekeeper. He was the sheriff of sorts though he had no formal connection with law and order as such apart from catching poachers,

225

and the police drove through his fief rarely if ever. There was no crime and any miscreants would be treated to shotgun justice.

Next door lived Nigel, a Harley Davidson enthusiast. I didn't dislike motorbikes when we arrived but by the time we moved I did.

The village was actually idyllic. The kids could play out with total safety, there was as I say no crime and we were befriended by Peter the Estate Manger and his wife Elaine, Mrs Cooper, one time housekeeper at the big house and by those more respectable denizens of the 'Land that time forgot' as we called it. I could not have chosen a better place to bring up my burgeoning family.

When we moved, Mrs McLoughlin travelled with Pat to unpack while I went on ahead to meet the removals people. As they travelled from Boroughbridge, just two miles from the village along deserted country lanes, Pat and her mother discussed whether the essentials of life could be found. It was as if they were in a foreign, third world land. I had to remind them that there were in fact supermarkets nearby just like Liverpool.

A year later when we had settled and become more accustomed to the pace of life my mother in law visited. The village had a small shop cum post office and a pub. She said to Pat,

*'Ill go and get some milk,'*

*'No there won't be any today it only comes Tuesday and Thursday.'* Replied my wife.

Pat senior was perplexed and was reinforced in her view we had abandoned civilisation for the wild west.

Yorkshire schools were many times times better than those in Merseyside at that time. They are probably a thousand times better

now. Skelton had its own school to go with the shop, pub and church. The school was in the gift of the estate and the governors consisted of an ancient and very irascible vicar we nicknamed the 'Miserable' Stirk; Peter the Estate manager and the headmistress. The teaching post was a sinecure and because of the size of the school the headmistress was also the teacher (plus another part time teacher). When the law changed and parent governors were required, I was invited onto the Governors, together with Nigel's, wife who was a nurse.

The school consisted of a single large room typical of Victorian rural schools and there were just eighteen children between the ages of four and eleven. During our time there this went down to just twenty children, of which four belonged to me at one stage.

The school did plenty of activities and I even helped out running the school football team, seven kids, all ages, both boys and girls, pitted against similarly small rural competition across a wide area.

The school didn't do too badly though and both Lenny and Lizzy passed the eleven-plus test to go to Ripon Grammar school. The highlight of the year as far as the village was concerned was the annual Gala where there were races, fancy dress competitions and of course the tent and cake, flower and small animal classes. At the end of the long summer day there was dancing and festivities long into the night.

The kids also went to the Church of England Sunday school which was part of the institutions of the village. My kids, Nigel's two who were similar age, Peter's two (only occasionally) and the two Palins who lived next door but one and whose parents were also our friends attended regularly. It was run by an old lady Mrs Renton who was a retired maths teacher, very odd but one of the institutions herself. She was like a teacher from St Trinians. From another age.

There was no Catholic church in Skelton, so we went to a tiny chapel of ease in nearby Minskip where we got to know the tiny Catholic community of farmers very well. Cannon Parker, the priest from Ripon covered the chapel for a single Sunday mass and I took my turn at reading the lessons. Cannon Parker was an Engish priest who told us he had been in Rome for a long time at the English College (a Catholic university there) for many years before coming back to Yorkshire in semi retirement. He lived in the Ripon Presbytery with his sister who might have been his twin, she was very like him and we laughed that they were really the same person, we rarely saw them together. Shades of the Bates motel!

My faith changed over these years. It hit a flashpoint when I was in church reading the bidding prayers for that day – and my two values of Catholicism and patriotism met head-on. That very morning, British soldiers had died in a bombing in Ulster. Without thinking to check with the priest, I added their names to the prayer list I read out.

The priest was not happy! I felt uncomfortable that he felt uncomfortable. Those soldiers who died at the hands of the IRA had been serving their country – the country where I now prayed for them. My faith in the Catholic church and its representatives was hit that day and lessened further when the priest wouldn't engage in any form of theological discussion with me when we had had the chance. I'd considered myself a cultured Catholic – all those years with the Jesuits, after all. Surely, his job was to debate and discuss with an interested believer! I still considered it my duty to bring the kids up as Catholics until they could decide their paths for themselves but for myself, it was a watershed from which I have never recovered.

The quality of the schools and the idyllic nature of our country lifestyle meant there was no question of my growing family returning to Liverpool when my secondment ended in 1991. By this time we had five, Kate was born in Harrogate Hospital in October 1989 and by the time I was due to return to Liverpool in July of 1991 Pat was once again pregnant with Edward my sixth and last child born in the

October of that year when I was already working back in Liverpool, only coming home on my rest days and struggling with my latest posting.

Belle Vale was the worst posting I ever had and I hated it with a passion. I returned as an Inspector of three years standing and I suppose didn't help myself. As far as I was concerned I was

experienced, yet I had never served operationally in the rank. Furthermore I had been in the rarified environment of the CPU. I was the 'Taliban' and had wielded a lot of power within the training estate even on those of a higher rank than me. I represented the future, and was terribly woke and sanctimonious for the time. To the operational policing world I may have had two heads.

It was made clear from day one that I was 'newly promoted' as far as they were concerned and I needed to get off my high horse and fit in. The division I went to included Belle Vale and Garston which I covered, Speke where I had been in the CID you may remember and Toxteth which still policed a diverse and simmering population.

I knew how modern policing should be theoretically and ideologically, especially in a potential crucible like Toxteth, and it didn't include the Garston Globe. This was an unofficial internal publication part comedy part satire produced surreptitiously by a secret cabal on the photocopier. Several hundred copies were produced each moth and the 'editorial team' continually pushed the boundaries of good taste with a mixture of pornography, libel and puerile humour. Utter filth.

The first episode I experienced had a cover of a Ku Klux Klan meeting with participants labelled as various senior officers. It was both dangerous in a reputational sense and actually offended me but the more I pushed back the more I was taunted by copies, in my in-tray, in my locker, in my office drawer. Eventually I found out the brains behind it, It was the Chef Superintendent of the division and his deputy. I was flogging a dead horse and my fighting against it had done me nothing but personal harm.

The whole sub division was a huge clique and I had failed the initial test to join it and had become an outsider. My only hope was to escape somehow. Unlike my Days and EP experience I had no minder. I was living at my mums and she treated me as if I had never been away and was still seventeen, and then there was Ian ever present and prowling all night. In the middle of the night I would wake to find him standing in the doorway staring at me.

Things came to a head in work one night when I stopped a drunk driver in the wee small hours only for it to be the divisional deputy commander. I should have arrested him really but the consequences would have been dire. As it was a few days later I left the station in my battered mini metro, anything else would have been inviting theft staying in Cantril Farm. As I turned left on my way home my wheel flew off and bounced down the road. Someone had removed the wheel nuts.

Was I tempted to leave? I am not that stupid! I had invested more than fifteen years in my career. I soldiered on, never diluting my principles with the trash that went on around me. It was time to go though and I pulled in every contact I could think of resulting in an offer to go to the Force Control Room. I jumped at it. Into the fire indeed as it turned out.

My move was a case of go, escape, sort out the details later. The responsibility and pressure of this role were enormous. Out of hours, I was the most senior person on duty in Merseyside. Each Friday at 6 p.m., a boat loaded with enough chlorine to destroy Liverpool sailed with the tide. As control room inspector, should the ship be hijacked, have an accident or a leak, my orders could save or kill thousands. This was only one of countless hazards I was responsible for listed in the contingency plans.

When I arrived I realised that I was there largely because they were desperate for staff. It wasn't a popular job for Inspectors and very much a buyers market. Once you were in though the boot was firmly on the other foot and it was practically impossible to leave.

233

Before I accepted the offer (though given my standing in Belle Vale it was not really a decision for me) I impressed on the Chief Inspector Communications my domestic circumstances.

*'I can work as long as you want every shift, twelve hours or more a day, but I MUST have my days off otherwise I will end up divorced.'*

*'Oh that's no problem,'* he said, *'as long as you are prepared to work overtime on your shifts that's great you're just what I need.'*

*'When do I start then said I, as soon as possible I hope.'* A week later I was there.

### First shift

*"Ah Lenny isn't it, I'm Frank, just checking you're ok to work all your rest days this week and next?"*

*No Frank, has Richie not told you, I live in Yorkshire and can't work rest days, but pencil me in for Overtime every shift.'*

*'But you have to work rest days otherwise the rest of us won't be able to cope.'*

*'Sorry, no, speak to Richie, he'll explain.'*

Next day

*'Len,'* says Richie the Chief Inspector. *'I understand you won't work your rest days, you've got to.'*

*'No we agreed if you remember'*

*'You've got to.'*

*'No, you can order me to but you'll have to give e 28 days notice'*

*'Don't be a smart arse.'* He said.

## INTO THE FIRE INDEED.

A month and two worked rest days later, and the next eight already rostered, I was once more called into Richie's office.

*'I have had a phone call from the Chief Constables Office. They tell me you are getting transferred to the Force Re-organisation Team. I've told them I can't let you go till you find me a replacement.'*

I was faced with a problem. A plumb job in the Chief Constables office but who would I find? That night I went to visit Mrs McLoughlin who had not been well and I had to drive past the Anfield football ground. There was a match on and I spotted John, an Inspector I knew from the CPU.

*'Hi John, how goes it,'*

*'Oh Great, what are you doing now?'*

*'I'm Force Control room Inspector,'*

*'Really, is there much overtime?'*

John was perpetually hard up and, though married to an occupational therapist had a string of affairs for which he needed a continual supply of money.

*'John, it's amazing as much overtime as you can work, unlimited.'*

*'How do I get a job there then,'*

*'Actually John I hear there is a vacancy coming up do you want me to put a good word in?'*

*'Oh that would be great, thanks, I owe you one,'*

**SO IN ONE BOUND I WAS FREE!**

# God's Country

**'One ewe tomorrow true**
**Two ewes aplenty**
**Three oh, how happy we**
**Four nearly gentry.'**
('Sheep Counting' – John Tams)

*'That will be £638 please sir,'*
said the very polite lady behind
the counter in the Northallerton
Auction Mart.

*'Sorry, my name is Gill, there*
*must be some mistake'*

*'No, no mistake sir, eleven*
*Yorkshire Mule ewes with lambs*
*at foot, £638.'*

*'But I didn't buy eleven I only bought one with two lambs,'* I said,
a little irritated now and feeling that I was being diddled.

*'Did you bid on lot 34,'*

*'Yes that's right,'* I said

'*Have you ever been to an auction before,* 'the lady said kindly, as if speaking to a small child now.

'*Actually no, this is my first time.*'

'*OK, that probably explains it, the way it works is that when you bid, you bid for everything that is in the ring on that lot.*'

'*But the man definitely said £58, the farmer who briefed me said £55 was too cheap, and £60 was too much, that's why I bid £58.*'

'*Yes and he was right, look, you bid £58 per sheep there were eleven sheep that's £638, the lambs are included. At an auction once the hammer goes down you've bought them, its not like a shop. Sorry but they're yours now.*'

'*But I don't know how I'll get them home, I've only got a Fiesta,*' I said forlornly but with a sense of panic rising within me. I feel very silly.

'*Oh don't worry, I'll tell Albert, out the back, he's got a lorry and he'll deliver them for £20, you live local I suppose,*'

'*Yes Gatenby.*'

'*OK give me your address and I'll sort Albert out, you will have to pay him cash on delivery, and here is £1 per sheep luck money.*'

'*What's that,*'

*'Well it ensures good luck, you get it from the seller, There you go it only cost you £57 in the end then eh,'*

She laughed and I wrote out a cheque for an amount I couldn't really afford and had not expected; and pocketed the eleven pound coins luck money though I didn't feel very lucky, not sure what I was going to do when the sheep arrived.

But, dear reader, time to climb back aboard the TARDIS and to 1991 again. You will recall our hero had just escaped from the Force Control Room courtesy of John my erstwhile CPU colleague.

I wouldn't feel too sorry for John however. He loved it when he got there and made a fortune in overtime until the regulations were changed in 1995 and Inspectors pay was consolidated. He never never did escape though and retired in post, one wife lighter.

Within 72 hours of my chance meeting at Anfield I was arriving at Stanley Road Police Station, temporary home of the Force

Reorganisation and Implementation Team (FRIT for short). I think a short history lesson may be useful here.

As I mentioned earlier in this tome, Merseyside Police was formed in 1974 from a number of smaller forces, and pieces of Lancashire and Cheshire Constabularies. This was part of the largest reorganisation of Police Forces in the twentieth century.

Before 1974, what became Merseyside had been covered by a number of borough forces, Birkenhead, Wallasey, Bootle, Southport, St Helens as well as Liverpool City. All these forces were headed by their own Chief Constables and had full infrastructures. In addition two Lancashire Divisions and one Cheshire Division each headed by a Chief Superintendent and his (there were only men then) infrastructure were added to the city and boroughs.

These then were organised into a Merseyside Police Force of twelve Divisions each headed by a Chief Superintendent, five Superintendents, ten Chief Inspectors, twenty Inspectors and a full complement each of bobbies and sergeants.

To contrast this with today, Merseyside Police has an Inspector roughly covering what was a Superintendent's post in 1974.

FRIT's job in 1991 was the first reorganisation since the force was established and was an interim point toward the streamlined (some might say ineffective) organisation we have today and I must bear some blame for today's sorry state of affairs, yet the interim model we came up with in my view did work and further reorganisations should have stopped there.

The team we had was headed by Geoff my minder from Training, assisted by a cadaverous extremely tall Superintendent called Frank, who was married appropriately to the Coyne Funeral Directors heiress and retired to be a funeral director which he suited down to the ground complete with top hat.

I won't bore you with the details of our re-organisation except to say we broke up the existing Divisions and this had the pleasing (and not co-incidental) effect of breaking up the cabal which was F Division (Belle Vale etc.) and forcing those senior offices who were in my view a disgrace upon the service into early retirement. We, (I), replaced them with a more appropriate breed of leader and the days of the Garston Globe, Toxteth Times, Speke Sentinel and their ilk were committed to the dustbin of history, and good riddance.

My time on FRIT helped me domestically. My hours were very flexible, I got lots of overtime but when it suited me, a mobile phone that was as big as a briefcase and I felt a little better off. I still lived with Mum and Ian but was able to go home midweek as well as weekends and when summoned by Mr Postlethwaite, the deputy head of Ripon Grammar school to tell me Lenny had been fighting and was suspended again. Though it didn't affect Lenny too much as he was still in the Rugby team so that forgave literally a multitude of sins.

What FRIT did most for me though was get me noticed again and after two years, in which for some obscure reason the Assistant Chief Constable thought I had a Masters degree in Mathematics from Oxford (of which I didn't disabuse him), I was selected to return to CPU as a Chief Inspector in charge of the Curriculum Design department.

So as 1994 I once more returned to God's Country and the bosom of my family in Skelton. I was to remain in Yorkshire for a glorious six years. We were happy there and both Pat and I still think it is the finest place to live in all of the UK.

I inherited, as usual a dysfunctional department which needed cleaning. My new boss Stuart, himself only recently appointed had previously been a student on my Evaluation Course. He was likeable and able but coasting to retirement and looking for an easy life.

I had a mixed team of sixteen Police Inspectors and Civil Servants who researched and wrote training materials to form the curricula of courses for those up to and including Chief Inspector.

I relatively quickly identified three trouble makers among the Police staff and replaced them within months resulting in a much more functional team. The civil servants however were there for the duration and subject to civil service regulations which once more served to improve my experience and education in management and manipulation.

Within days of my arrival one of the civil servants, a retired regularly army Captain who had become a Territorial Army Major in his spare time confronted me.

*'You can't give me any orders, I outrank you, I'm a Major.'*

I did point out that his spare time commitment was different from his day job which wasn't in the military but it took considerable effort to manage the man who was mad as a 'March Hare'.

I eventually solved the problem by taking a leaf out of Tommy Hall's playbook and got him moved to a nice job at the Police College in Bramshill, where he felt more important and was someone else's problem.

Over the following years we became quite a slick operation I think. Our courses were designed following requests from the various committees of the Association of Chief Police Officers (ACPO), called something else these days I understand. I would attend these committees to be given instructions when summoned, or present the results of training needs analyses (TNAs) and other research. The committees also included staff association representatives and I got to know them well and came to respect the Police Federation's role within the service.

As our reputation improved we also received requests for TNAs or courses from other arms of government and the security services and I was asked to give presentations or attend conferences abroad. Pat and I had a very nice break in Vienna as a result (I paid for her obviously).

By this time Les Poole had retired and been replaced by Bernard Whyte, an Assistant Chief Constable from Cambridge who was a quiet unassuming man clearly selected as a peacemaker now the system was embedded and after the fiery days of Les and his 'Taliban'.

Bernard seemed to like me, I think it was helped by the fact that he and his wife were devout catholics with five children, now grown up so had some fellow feeling with us. He was a member of the Catenian Association which is a Catholic Society for professional men. Membership is very restricted and by invitation only. Bernard invited me to join under his sponsorship which is a very great honour. Unfortunately I was, and still am not a lover of what I regard as secret societies, I suppose it's now in built in me, so I politely declined though I'm sure it would have benefitted me greatly had I accepted.

He chose me to accompany him on an official visit to evaluate the Police training system in Greece on behalf of the Foreign Office. It was a splendid visit. On arrival we were allocated a personal liaison officer who was a Colonel in the Greek National Police and a personal tour guide, the same guide that had been allocated the previous week to the Clintons, so I felt very important.

In fairness my job was to do most of the research and the Colonel and I travelled around the country interviewing but mainly visiting the sites of ancient Greece and enjoying lavish banquet meals at the expense of the Greek Police. As far as the policing issues were concerned though the Colonel was very forthright and helpful. I arranged with him to go on patrol around the greater Athens area at different times of the day.

## Night Patrol

*'So what are the main crime issues here,'*

*'Oh Burglary and car theft.'*

*'So what are the causes?'*

*'It's the Albanians, Greek people are very honest.'*

## Afternoon Patrol

*'Well it is very run down and seedy, prostitution and Drugs'*

*'It's the Albanians, Greek people are very moral, they wouldn't do that sort of thing. It will never get better till we get rid of the Albanians.'*

So I came away with the impression that the Greek Police were very racist and the main training issue was diversity input.

In the last decade however I have had a lot more to do with European policing and organised crime investigation. In hindsight maybe the Colonel was absolutely correct. But my report stood anyway and nicely fitted in with the agenda of both the UK and EU. It would be something that would give me brownie points later on.

SOUTH WALES POLICE

AUSTRALIA
V
FRANCE

SATURDAY 6.11.99

ADMIT: C/INSP GILL

SIGNED:....................
EVENT COMMANDER/CO-ORDINATOR

TO BE PRODUCED WITH
WARRANT CARD

A major slice of our design work related to Major event planning and managing public disorder and with some jiggery pokery I managed to get permission to observe the Major Event Planning and implementation of the Rugby World Cup at the Millennium Stadium in Cardiff in uniform. Watching the match from the Police Control room and the pitch side.

By the end of 1994 I was tasked with a project which was eventually to pay me big dividends in terms of the contacts I needed to move on after I retired.

When the Rwandan civil war finished in July 1994 the UK government's contribution to reconstruction was twofold. Under the leadership of the Overseas Development Agency (ODA) and Clare Short we provided one thousand bicycles (yes you read it correctly) and a police training course in British Neighbourhood Policing. Not the response you may have first thought of to a nation where inter-tribal violence had led to the deaths of 800,000 people in central Equatorial Africa.

Nonetheless the CPU (my team) were tasked with the course design and I was made project manager to employ consultants, design the training and implement a delivery programme. This was to prove one of the most personally valuable jobs I had ever had in the end though I didn't know it at the time.

My work life at the CPU settled quickly into a nice routine and I had the ability to work flexibly and from home when necessary. Though I needed to travel, mainly to London for meetings, most of the time I was in Harrogate and I was therefore able to concentrate on helping Pat bring up our now substantial family of six. Across six productive, satisfying years, I combined the work I enjoyed with providing a stable home for the family as they progressed to secondary school and beyond.

Lenny I have alluded to already. He was at the Grammar school and began to play rugby when he started. To help him improve I also took him to Harrogate Rugby Club where he was one of the stalwarts of the team. He was big lad for his age and played at number 8 which is a key position and a much sought after role at the back of the scrum. Together we went on a couple of rugby tours which I helped arrange.

On one occasion using my IPA contacts I arranged a tour to the Dublin Area. Through a variety of fund raising wheezes we kept the costs down to practically zero and had a fine time with the boys and some of the more dedicated dads in tow. Despite losing almost all the matches, they were very good the Irish, we had a splendid time.

Due to some misunderstanding on the part of our host though, one Kevin from the Irish Special Branch (or it may have been his hangover) we missed the return boat and a keystone cops odyssey ensued from Dublin to Dún Laoghaire where Kevin and I had to convince the Ferry Captain we were an official Police team (the thirteen year olds trying to look a lot older than they were and failing). Our special pleading worked however and the ferry captain kindly got us in ahead of schedule and we caught the connecting train (just). I dread to think how much extra fuel it cost the ferry company for us to arrive an hour ahead of schedule though the passengers were pleased.

As Len got older, his rugby improved enormously. By the time he was sixteen it was time to enter the arcane representative system. At that age the private schools have representative sport sown up. Having been excluded as a result of 'communications errors' about a north Yorkshire trial, (they never told us the time or venue). It took a phone call.

*'Hello is that Ashville College. Can I speak to Mr .....'*

*'Oh I'm afraid he's not available, can I pass on a message.'*

*'Yes, its Chief Inspector Gill from the Police can you ask him to ring me as a matter of urgency.'*

Three minutes later

*'Hello, Chief Inspector Gill, it's Mr ...... from Ashville'*
*'Oh Yes its about the North Yorkshire Trial, there are boys from Ripon Grammar School eligible. Can you give me the time and venue.'*

*'Oh is that all, Oh yes its this evening at Ashville.'*

*'Thanks, see you then.'*

Lenny got selected for North Yorkshire that night, then at two more levels and finally, the magical selection. The Yorkshire team.

We arrived at the usual cold, damp clubhouse, lads and dads, coaches and stray families hanging round queuing to book in for the trial.

We stand back listening. Most of those booking in are going for the sexy positions, Flankers, number 8, fly half, full back. Lenny plays number 7, (a flanker) he will be one of more than ten at this trial and some of them look very good, a couple are definitely England material we hear.

I have a brainwave, no-one wants to play in the front row. I push him forward,

'Gill; Leonard Gill,' I say to the man booking them in intently looking at his list'

A quick upside down scan reveals no hookers (number two).

'Ah yes,' says the man, 'Leonard Gill: number seven.'

'No number two I say, it's a misprint, 2, 7 they look the same.'

*'Oh OK, that's good, he's the only hooker.'*

Success, he got selected. England here we come.

It was a busy time for all of us, those years in the mid nineties. Dancing and Brownies in Boroughbridge and Pinkies for Vicky and Sarah when they weren't old enough (we made that up of course to keep them happy). Violin lessons for Liz and Guitar for Vix. Pat was out every night and did a night shift at the weekend to make ends meet so the time flew by and the kids grew up so fast.

Pat also started studying. An access course led to a degree at Ripon and York St John College. She started studying a history and heritage course but inevitably ended up doing marketing as Universities followed the money.

Sports wise Lizzy began athletics so we found a club in
Richmond, a long way to travel but it was her preferred sport as she
never really took to teams, she was a very good sprinter and jumper
for both length and height. She was always a very talented girl, music,
sport and learning coming naturally she excelled at just about
everything she tried but quickly tired of things and would never stick
at it.

Of course Vicky wanted to be included too and to be different we
steered her toward throwing, shot putt and javelin like me, she was
actually remarkably fast at 100 metres too though she ran like Michael
Johnson barely lifting her feet up. Vicky's great strength was and is
her ability to stick at things. Even if she wasn't initially a star she
persisted. By the time she was sixteen she represented the East of
England at Athletics and the North of England at Netball where she
had become one of the stars of the team at school.

**Friday, October 10, 1997**

### Six of the best

NO fewer than six St John Fisher School pupils have been selected for the North Yorkshire County squad.

Sixth-former Jessica Hughes has been picked for the U-19s squad, Katherine Williams and Emily Maguire the U-16s and Philippa Tindall, Vicky Gill and Rachel Thompson the U-14s.

To top that off, Emily and Katherine will be at the trials for the England squad in Huddersfield this weekend.

PE teacher Sheridan Jones said: "Over the last few years we have only been having one or two players selected for the county netball sides.

"But that has been on the increase and to get six is credit not only to the girls but the whole school's effort to the sport."

■ CAP THAT. From left to right, Katherine Williams, Rachel Thompson, Emily Maguire, Vicky Gill and Philippa Tindall, who have all received county honours. (A18467c)

We did our best during those years to get abroad on holiday every
year. We went to France camping more than once, the kids jammed

254

in the back of my cavalier while I had it and after it had blown up a 7 seat Peugeot 505 which made things considerably more comfortable.

That car took us safely on a tour to the Benelux countries armed with snow chains borrowed from Sandy, the local garage owner in Ripon who also ran the judo club where the three oldest went every week.

In 1994 Mrs McLoughlin sadly passed away following a melanoma which spread. We were all devastated, she had helped us a lot over the years and the kids were very close to her. She did though leave us a small legacy which enabled us all to go to Euro-Disney, a lavish holiday by our standards.

We also tried to reward Lenny and Lizzie after their GCSE exams with a holiday that they didn't have to share with anyone else. Lenny plumped to go with me on an adventure holiday to Egypt, an eye opener for us both, while two years later Pat repeated the exercise with Lizzy when both went to Malaysia. The only thing I remember about that trip was spending hours on the telephone trying to arrange an emergency credit card for them when they were robbed in the Langkawi hotel grounds, fortunately both were okay and received VIP service from the local Police when they found out I was a senior policeman myself. After that trip we ran out of cash though to take the others away in similar fashion.

Secondments usually last for three years, hence my return from my first stint at Harrogate in 1991. However by 1997, when my second secondment was up, I was asked by the management to extend a further three years. In purely career terms it was probably the equivalent of shooting myself in the foot. I had been a temporary Chief Inspector during my time at CPU and a return to an operational role would have almost certainly assured a promotion to

Superintendent by the time I was due to retire in 2006. For me though it was not straightforward. The family were happy and stable in Yorkshire, Len and Lizzy were at Grammar School, Len in his last year before A Levels and Liz her last year before GCSEs. Vix was riding high in her sports and very happy at St John Fisher in Harrogate and the little ones settled at primary school. We had a good life, Pat was about to graduate and the family for me was everything. I worked to live I did not live to work.

I had also got into riding in a big way. Horses and dogs have always had a special place in my soul (Four Feather Falls you see!). As a small boy I was taken to the 'May Horse' heavy horse parades in Liverpool as mum's brothers were carters and kept heavy horses.

In Huyton , I would walk past a riding school in Huyton Lane several times a week and harass mum to let me have riding lessons but she never did.

I entered competitions almost every week trying to win a horse (such competitions proliferated in the 1960s) though had I won I don't know where I would have kept the animal; and in Maghull I finally learned to ride going to a riding school and getting the basics.

It was my deepest desire to own a horse and in 1997, having made the decision to stay I finally realised my wish. In Skelton I had flirted with riding, exercising a farmers horse a few times every week in nearby Boroughbridge, and I began to take the older kids riding every weekend when Pat was sleeping after nights to keep them out of her way. I found a lovely riding school in Pateley Bridge and, as is normal with these establishments, regular attendance meant getting sucked into extra activities. I made an arrangement with a local farmer there

to exercise his Shire Horses (easy to ride but not very comfortable)
and the owner of the stable, Jane encouraged me to enter show
jumping events she and friends organised.

As I got more more involved I rode the same horse all the time,
Pye, a piebald gelding like a gypsy horse which I was able to throw
around the show jumping course nimbly winning several
competitions to the chagrin of the green welly and pony club set.
Eventually I decided to buy Pye but was unable to come to a sensible
arrangement with the owners but as luck would have it was able to
reach a long loan agreement with a local businessman who had a fine
Black Irish Hunter called Scartine after the Irish Hunt of that name.

It gave me satisfaction that my children enjoyed what I'd wanted
most in my childhood but hadn't believed I could access. Looking
back now, riding lessons wouldn't have been beyond my family's

reach. It's just that there had been the assumption they weren't for families 'like ours'. Here, in no time at all, we all became quite good!

Incredibly, 'home' had recently become an amazing 600-acre country seat in Gatenby, a small north Yorkshire village near Bedale.

It was not the typical habitat of a Merseyside police inspector, even one halfway through a further three-year posting with the Home Office in Harrogate. But then, where's the fun in typical?

It was obvious to me that the extension would not be repeated and by the millennium I would have to return to Merseyside. We had put our house up for sale and had had almost no interest so I decided that I needed to sell now at whatever price I could get and move to rented accommodation for what remained of my secondment. I wasn't paying after all. The same constraints however remained as when I had arrived. I needed a big house and was loathe to go back to an urban environment. I approached Peter, the estate manager who we were very friendly with.

*'Oh, I'll have a look and put some feelers out,'* he said.

In the event he came up with three possibilities, all of which were very attractive. I had a ceiling of £600 a month allowance and didn't really want to add my own money. In the event I decided on Allerthorpe Hall. This was and remains my dream home. It was built in 1608 and was a grade one listed building which other people have told us was very haunted but it clearly liked us because we were never bothered and even welcomed into its heart. In addition as a result of some archaic feudal quirk we even had the sole right to use a civil war era covered pew in the local church.

The music room as we called it, the oldest room in the house like that in the painting by Yeames *'When did you last see your father?'*, was, I must admit spooky, though I am not really sensitive. It always seemed as if something was there benignly watching me. We ushered the Millennium in, in that room having a family party, just the family

and the ghosts as the year 2000 landed. I hope they enjoyed it. I played the tin whistle and the bodhrán drum after a fashion and wonder if similar festivities happened in that same space to celebrate

the end of the civil war, the Restoration or the defeat of the Jacobites. My romantic self would like to think so.

The only drawback was that it was on a pig farm so there was noise once a week at 4am when the pigs would be loaded aboard trucks destined for the abattoir. Apart from that it was idyllic though Pat never took to it because there were so many rooms to clean and tidy; it wore her out.

## And so to sheep!

I came back that day from the Northallerton auction mart in a lather. I had asked Albert, the delivery man to take his time while I sorted the field out. The house had a half acre orchard and I needed the sheep to eat the grass as I only had an electric fly-mo and it had packed in with the long grass growing like topsy in the summer heat.

Frantically, helped by Lenny I went and bought rolls of pig wire, fence posts, a post driver and nails and erected a makeshift fence in about two hours. Just before the lorry arrived with my new charges.

Dripping with sweat we confined them to the orchard and I paid the van driver. The whole episode had cost me over one thousand pounds. A ride-on mower would have been cheaper.

The owner of the pig farm became quite friendly and let me have shooting and grazing rights for £1 a year and I rented a six acre field behind the house for another £1 a year as our flock grew with the addition of two pet lambs, Cuthbert and Heather, some Jacob sheep and a few Herdwicks as well as a fine Jacob ram we called Charlie who I bought from the Masham sheep fair and brought home in the back of the fiesta, little Edward holding him all the way.

Next we acquired a half dozen chickens and housed them in the semi derelict outhouses. Bonnie, sadly long passed on, had been replaced by now by another small border collie called Thistle and a rescued flat coat retriever called Holly who we had to thank for saving Lenny's life while we were in Skelton. He fell asleep in his bed, the electric light fell down and set fire to the bedclothes. Hollie dragged him out of bed and made such a racket we came in and extinguished the smouldering bed cover. Thank goodness for Holly.

We had fun with the livestock though and learned lots of animal husbandry skills. Pat even used her midwifery training in subsequent years when we lambed successfully. It was a great life. The happiest I have ever been I think. Sheep and chicken rearing, making cider from the abundant apples , shooting and fishing. And all without the bother of neighbours. Bliss.

There was just one cloud on our otherwise idyllic existence at Allerthorpe. Katherine was seven when we moved and she went to St Wilfrid's Primary School in Ripon. I suspect that certain parents who had been friendly with us thought we had won the lottery or something and were very jealous of our new house. When we were not forthcoming (because we hadn't won the lottery of course) whatever they said between themselves translated itself into bullying and social exclusion of Kate at school. It made her very unhappy and depressed and though we complained to the school they and the priest proved unequal to the task and we dipped into our own limited savings and switched her to the private Queen Mary's School situated between Ripon and Bedale which went well. Despite this, for my other five children and me especially – those years remain among our happiest.

Like Katherine, Sarah and Edward attended St Wilfrid's primary school but they both had different personalities to Kate. Sarah had a best friend, Claire and together they blithely sailed through the world unaware of social slights and bullying.

By 1999 Sarah followed Vicky to St John Fisher Catholic High School in Harrogate and, if they wanted to arrive on time they caught the bus in a nearby village at 7 am for the 2 hour journey to school. More often though I took them both on my way to work and they were invariably late and had many a harsh word from the deputy head but he eventually gave up. They were after all model pupils in other respects though Sarah never took to the school as Vix had.

Edward had two 'best friends', Sam and Gregory. Greg's parents were between houses and we agreed that they could temporarily stay with us as the house was so big, (we had 9 bedrooms in all, 4 living rooms and 2 kitchens). It was intended to be a very short term arrangement but they stayed for more than a year and took over tenancy of the house when we left.

Living the country dream at Allerthorpe (from 1996 until 2000) was among my life highlights. So many life events took place there. Lenny left to study Archeology at Durham University and from there, to Sandhurst and the Green Howards.

In 1999 I have a vivid memory. Floods abound in North Yorkshire and Allerthorpe Hall is cut off surrounded on all sides stretching over 100 yards of flooded lanes and fields.

Lizzy is in the middle of her 'A' Levels, Vicky her GCSEs.

Panic, tantrums, stamping of feet. They can't miss their exams, their futures depend upon it, what are we going to do?, Can we do anything?

Outside the beeping of a horn, the local farmer had his largest tractor and both girls stand on the running boards as they plough axle deep through the floods and onto the main road where friends have responded to our cry for help and take them to their dates with destiny.

Both were successful. Liz went to Newcastle to study Classics, Vix got into 6th form and two years later joined Lenny at Durham to study Sociology and into the army with an Officer's bursary thanks in no small part to her sporting success.

By mid 1999, it was all change at the CPU. Bernard Whyte in his turn had retired and the Unit merged into a larger organisation, 'National Police Training' based at the Police College in Bramshill Hampshire, the CPU was under threat of closure. And the writing was on the wall for me.

In 1988 I had been the future, a change agent. By 1999, I was the old guard like the Instructors I had replaced. I was a minority voice opposing the incoming regime as a retrograde step and my views were hastening my departure.

In preparation I started house hunting. We still had our animals and we had taken to the rural life so I settled on a farmhouse with a little land in Wales which was in a woeful state of repair. I had intended to work on the house at the weekends until mid 2000 but when I returned to work in January of that year after the Christmas break the new millennium had a nasty surprise. The axe fell on me swiftly and brutally. My secondment was terminated and I was back to Merseyside by the end of the month.

**Our Yorkshire idyll was over.**

# Cymru Am Byth?

**'Heartbeat, why do you miss when my baby kisses me?**
**Heartbeat, why does a love kiss stay in my memory?'**
(Heartbeat – TV Series Theme)

*'Oh hello Len, this is Rhian, she is from the village committee,'*

Pat introduced a neat, professional looking woman who later tells me she is a teacher.

*'She has come to invite us to the party in the village hall for the bank holiday. Isn't that lovely.'*

*'Oh hello, I am pleased to meet you.'* I am still in uniform, from work, it is a lovely sunny day in early summer. The Queen's Golden Jubilee is a couple of weeks away the first weekend in June 2002.

*'Yes',* she says, *'we are having a party for the bank holiday.'* I am a little confused about which bank holiday so I say,

*'Oh, what the Queens's Jubilee?'*

*'No the Bank Holiday weekend,'*

*'Yes The Jubilee weekend?'*

*'We prefer to just refer to it as the Bank Holiday here,'* she replies,
*'We don't recognise the English Queen, we have our own royal family
descended from Owain Glyndwr.'*

This was not the first time we were confronted with such attitudes on
our move to Wales (which the kids believed was just another county of
England and were quickly disabused of the fact)

In August of 2000, just a couple of months after properly moving in,
Pat had secured a job at Denbigh Infirmary and wanted to raise the
Union Jack to celebrate the Queen Mother's 100th birthday.

*'Where do you keep the flag,'* she asked a colleague

*'Oh its in the chest over there,'*

Getting the Union Jack out to take it to the flagpole she is challenged
by her colleague, *'What are you doing with that, put it away quickly,'*

*'Why? Len says we should fly the flag today it's an official day.'*

*'Oh no she says I thought you meant the Welsh flag, they'll burn it
down if you put that up.'*

That same day the Union Jack flying outside Denbigh Police station
was indeed set ablaze. No one was ever brought to book.

271

So, '*Here be Dragons*', isn't that the phrase. Moving to Wales was very different and has taken me many years to adapt to.

When the axe fell in January 2000, I was told to return to Merseyside forthwith and my 28 days notice waived That didn't suit me and there followed a telephone call to the Merseyside Police Federation and very soon after my Union Reps arrived. Together we launched a grievance and won a concession that the Home Office would continue to fund Allerthorpe Hall until the end of July of that year for Pat and the kids to live in, as long as I relinquished my role which was effectively made a redundant post in the re-organisation.

The housing arrangement was some consolation as there was still lots to do to bring my new farmhouse up to scratch. I had found it practically impossible to find local tradesmen and a friend, Mike who had been our plumber and electrician in Yorkshire for years offered to help me do the place up virtually at cost price.

I was the recipient of several kindnesses from the people of God's country. Mike lent me his van, so Pat could keep the car while I was away and the Pig farmer gave me free use of his horse box to save on removal costs, so, over the next four months I went to work during the day and worked until the early hours and every weekend; gutting the house and rebuilding it from the inside out.

Len helped too and brought a few of his mates from University to help me labour as we took down walls, put in new ones, replaced joists, floors and plaster till by the end of the school year it was fit for the family to relocate.

I brought some of the sheep with me in the trailer but the majority I sold at the Northallerton Auction (I was an old hand by now). I was joined by the family, or most of it. Len was at University of course but Lizzy decided she wasn't moving and stayed at Allerthorpe with our friends till it was time for her to go to Newcastle University.

The next problem was finding a suitable school. My research had not proved promising though my expectations were very high after a dozen years in Yorkshire and we really needed all the children to be in the same place after three years of them spread around North Yorkshire at various institutions.

Eventually I identified a semi independent Roman Catholic school which had a nice feeling and was willing to take all the children. The senior school of St Brigid's in Denbigh was a single sex girls school but the junior department was mixed and Edward was accepted there. The arrangement gave us a couple of years to get a better idea of local provision.

Once again though the Catholic church let me down and drove in the final nail to my allegiance. I asked the parish priest to endorse our application for travel assistance on denominational grounds. He refused and told me the kids should go to the Catholic sink school in either Rhyl or Wrexham, both of which were as bad as each other. I don't think my heart has been in Catholicism since.

When I moved into the house alone at the end of January the weather was very cold and wet. It rained every day. As I worked and the days grew longer I thought it wouldn't be long till the warmth of the long hot summers I had become used to in Yorkshire. But no. Yorkshire had very cold dry winters and hot dry summers, the operative word here is dry. Wales climate was very different. While the winter was a little warmer and the summer a little cooler it rained every day that first year at some point during the day for the first 135 days. I thought that I would have webbed feet by the end of the year.

While I worked into the early hours every night, renovating the house I resumed my career back in Merseyside. It was pot luck where I would end up; wherever a vacancy occurred; and travelling from Wales could have been a nightmare but my OSD network had not completely broken down. Paul my old Inspector from 1984 was now Divisional Commander in the Wirral and found me a place though it was supernumerary at first, such was the unexpectedness of my move. I started in Bromborough in a non-job but soon Paul prevailed on Ian the commander in Wallasey who also had responsibility for the Wirral control room and he appointed me head of communications.

It wasn't a job I relished after my experience in the Force Control Room but this time it was different. I was in charge and though the responsibility was greater in terms of performance and personnel management, I was much freer to come and go at my own discretion which facilitated my efforts at renovation and ensured I saw the family more often than could have been the case elsewhere. Once more though in hindsight it was a good move for me.

The problem with secondment to the home office, or anywhere else on the national stage, is that it gives one an overestimate of your own importance and value. Rubbing shoulders with Chief Constables and politicians on a daily basis is good for the ego but that ego gets inflated. Suddenly I was brought back to earth with a bump, just as I had been at Belle Vale years earlier. I was however humble enough at this point in my service to recognise the bump and put my shoulder to the wheel.

It was the the fuel dispute of September 2000 which did it. I was suddenly once more at the centre of the web controlling the crisis and briefing Ian several times a day to enable him to brief upward. He did well (ended up Assistant Chief Constable in North Wales) and so he quickly learnt to trust me and my personal credit went up.

After a year he made sure I was selected to lead the latest 'reorganisation' to restructure policing on the Wirral into a series of local neighbourhoods headed by Inspectors. So where there had been eight Superintendents in charge of Policing the Wirral when I joined in 1976, by the time our latest reorganisation was over in 2002 there were eight Inspectors.

The end of the reorganisation though led to the loss of my own top cover, Paul retired and Ian was promoted. Once more I stooped and started once more to build with my worn-out tools. The upshot was

275

that I was appointed to lead the community relations function, managing the Special Constabulary, creating policy and liaising with minorities the largest and most vociferous in Wirral being the Lesbian and Gay lobby, so I was also designated Gay Liaison Officer.

Though I dearly wanted to head one of the new Neighbourhoods the move forced me to indulge in a far more externally political environment with local politicians, Local Authority officers, pressure groups and the press. I can't say I found it difficult. I had weekends and most evenings off generally, and managed to delegate most of the work. This meant I could both have a better overview of the work and have time on my hands. As a result I was approached to stand for election as the Inspector's Union Representative a post I retained till my retirement in 2006. It also put me in a very strong lobbying position with the Force and Divisional management and a year later I was given my own command at last.

# Heswall.

Meanwhile we had settled into life in Wales. That first summer, once I got over my righteous monarchist outrage and the kids settled into school life with no help from the Catholic Church, the weather was lovely. It stopped raining at last and the school holidays stretched into long warm sunny days. I made a number of forays into the local community.

One of the sheep I brought with me was a Suffolk ram lamb we named Magnus. He was a magnificent creature and a giant by local Welsh standards who's sires tend to the mountain variety. Magnus was just a yearling by the summer of 2000 and, I decided to enter him for a local village agricultural show (sadly now a thing of the past since the foot and mouth epidemic of 2001 which destroyed local community shows). He won his class and it went some way in breaking the ice with a couple of my farmer neighbours.

The other foray was to Ruthin Rugby Club. Rugby is more a religion than a game in Wales and the club was a surefire way to integrate. It was not long before both Edward and Katharine were playing at junior level and we got to know a lot of people quickly.

I sought to repeat the successful tour I had arranged with Lenny in Harrogate, here in Ruthin. This time though the 'committee' decided on a tour to Edinburgh. Once more I threw myself into gaining sponsorship and we went on tour practically free. I had received vouchers from McDonalds for free food and a heavily discounted rate for accommodation and transport. On the way up Len, who was in the Army by now and posted to Catterick managed to find us accommodation and joined our little jaunt for a few days himself,

277

arranging a training experience with the Army representative team. Everyone was most impressed.

The final path to integration was of course school. St Brigids was an important way to settle into the area quickly and within a year Vicky, who had entered a small sixth form had been nominated as a finalist for Welsh woman of the year which was won eventually by Tanni Grey-Thompson that year so no disgrace there! Not bad for a girl who thought Wales was a large English county and could only speak a single sentence in Welsh as she had temporarily acquired a welsh boyfriend before the event.

St Brigids also had an active Combined Cadet form, a relic from its days as a private school and encouraged by the chair of Governors, a retired Colonel and local worthy. Vicky was somewhat of a find for them as she had already been awarded an Army bursary.

Back in Yorkshire, prior to GCSEs Vicky went to a careers day. She came back buzzing with a desire to join the army. I was dead against it but told her if she still wanted to join a year later I would support her. A year later she came to me and reminded me so off we went to the nearest Army Careers Office in Leeds. My stipulation was that she should enter officer training.

We arrived in our best bib and tucker and entered the office. Before us were three desks, army (a sergeant), navy (a Royal Marine sergeant) and the air force (a flight sergeant). Together we approached the army.

*'Hello. My daughter here is interested in joining the army as an officer.'* The man was non-plussed.

'Oh, we don't usually do Officers,' he said, 'Take a seat sir and I'll get the officer'. He scurried off up a set of stairs to the right.

Next minute a loud voice roared down the stairs,

'What the F***, Have we got a problem down there then!'

A few minutes later the sergeant came back looking a bit embarrassed and politely indicated we wait.

As we flicked through the grubby magazines scattered on the low table, a young lad of about seventeen came in. First off the mark was the Marine.

'Yes young man, come and sit here. Why do you want to join the marines lad?'

He replied seriously , 'Well Sergeant, I want to kill people.'

'You'll do for me, said the marine, here let's start filling in this form.'

Vicky and I exchanged a horrified look and at that moment a busy, slightly scruffy man with a moustache angrily emerged from the stairs and angrily burst into a small office opposite us. The sergeant nipped in behind him, and after raised voices came out and indicated we should go in.

'What's the problem then,' the little martinet wearing captain's insignia directed at me, ignoring my daughter.

'Hello, I said, and who might you be' I said.

279

He identified himself as a TA captain and I did likewise emphasising my own police rank. He swallowed visibly.

*'Lets start again shall we, Hello, my daughter here wishes to join the army as an officer.'*

It was so difficult, the process was both vague and arcane. He gave me the phone number of a colonel in York, I had a similar conversation with said colonel over the phone. Once again the private schools had youth entry sown up, he was a schools liaison officer but only to private schools it seemed.

Eventually, once I had pointed out Vicky's projected grades (which in fairness I inflated a bit) and told him she played representative sport at Regional level his attitude miraculously changed. The upshot was that following several more arcane stages Vicky was awarded an army sixth form scholarship which led to a bursary and a place at Sandhurst in the fullness of time.

She was now in the system but how hard it had been to get there and shatter the glass ceiling based, not on sex or race, but on schooling. It really amazed and shocked me. It's not what you know it's who you know that makes this country tick. We always wondered what happened to the putative murderer and the Royal Marines.

Heswall lies on the south west side of the Wirral peninsula. It is one of the top five richest parliamentary constituencies in England. To the north and west lies a similarly wealthy town called Hoylake, the home of a famous golf club. Both areas are nice, leafy semi rural places in which civilised people live. This area had once been commanded by a Superintendent, two Chief Inspectors and the whole resultant panoply of a Police sub division. In 2002 it was now commanded by an Inspector, two sergeants and around twenty officers.

The new Chief Superintendent Val had history with me, way back in my OSD days. He really wanted rid of me and gave Heswall to a young up and comer who, for reasons that still perplex me, soon realised he couldn't cope, had a minor nervous breakdown and was promptly transferred to a headquarters job in Liverpool. Poor Val was over a barrel and asked me if I would step in. I bit his hand off.

My days of emulating Z Cars, Hill Street Blues and such like were over. My favourite TV Cops were now the characters in Heartbeat. I chose to base myself at Heswall Police Station built in the late 1800s and formerly housing a full section and the home of the Sergeant and the Inspector in bygone days. It now lay on the rather busy high street surrounded by pleasant suburban shopkeepers and restaurants. I think, now that I have time to look back, that being the Sheriff of Heswall was the most enjoyable and rewarding posting in my career.

I was actually in command, proper command. Yes I had targets to
reduce crime and disorder and there was of course policy oversight
from the Divisional Commander but on a day to day basis I had both
tactical and strategic autonomy. My sergeant at Heswall was called
Barry. He had been posted along with me and replaced a younger
man. Barry was about 6 years older than me and had been a river pilot
before joining the Police and previously had a drink problem which
had caused people to avoid working with him. Val asked me if I would
have him and I agreed with a degree of trepidation. In the event he
was a great sergeant, sound, dependable and sensible. He renounced
drink and took to more esoteric interests collecting mood stones and
believing in ghosts though I don't think he went so far as turning to
God.

Ken was my sergeant at Hoylake. He was very tall and extremely odd
but had become an institution there and chairman of the sports and
social association. He was generally regarded as unmanageable and
had seen off several inspectors. I never really had an ounce of trouble
with him and was able to leave him to be the under-sheriff while I
concentrated on more strategic matters. I did make sure we went for
a drive across the sands once a week in the old 'landrover defender'
which I let him have as his personal toy and in which we had our
formal sessions in the privacy of the cab and devoid of witnesses.
Poor Ken eventually fell from grace as the victim of an online dating
scam where he lost his house and savings to a lady from Canada. After
that he was a broken man.

The section was like Pratchett's night watch, a collection of oddballs
who, despite their various weakness I harnessed to produce an
effective and happy section. Ronnie, who had been on the OSD with
me a long time ago had qualified as an electrician and was older and

282

wiser now. He had the problem beat and worked it well and effectively.

Mark lived down the very steep hill in Lower Heswall, on an estate of 1960s bungalows. I gave him what amounted to an old style unit beat based in his own house and he worked it on a mountain bike. He knew everyone and had no crime but fed in lots of intelligence.

Donna had been on my section in Tuebrook when she was a young girl and was useless then but she had hung in there and though lacking in drive was now very competent at paper work. I made her the traffic accident expert and called her the head of Road Policing.

Karl was a rough and ready guy who was sick of Liverpool and wanted a quiet life. I gave him a quiet little village to patrol on a bike with a very active neighbourhood watch. All very miss Marple. His strength was talking to people and smoothing their feathers. He was ideal and loved it.

Mark 2 and Neil were young and keen and wanted to lock people up, they reminded me of me twenty years before. They were my enforcers and I gave them free rein to act on intelligence from the others or at my direction. If we had a problem they sorted it and I supported them.

When I arrived, Heswall was short staffed. It wasn't a sought after posting and had the reputation of being for lazy time wasters. Within the year Barry and I had turned it around and every week I would receive a request from someone with a good reputation or a will to succeed to be posted to Heswall. Because I was also by now a senior member of the Federation though I reserved some spots for people with problems who I thought I could help, pulling them out of their despair.

Jimmy had a reputation for being lazy and slightly crazy and had a bad sick record. I took him on and called him the Station Manager and left him to organise things. He never had another day off while I was there.

Mike was a crazy. He had an anger management problem and was on the way to prosecution for assault. I decided to take him on too and after a series of heart to heart discussions I found his key. I promised him a Physical Training Instructor course (which I arranged through my contacts in Harrogate) if he would keep out of trouble and work on his anger. It worked. He wasn't my best man, but in the end he could be trusted.

I even managed to unofficially 'second' two traffic motorcyclists on a long loan which gave the good burghers of the parish the impression we had more resources than we really did. I could go on but you get the drift.

Val still didn't like me though and after about a year he moved me. Unfortunately the way I was set up involved an active media communications strategy which was unique in the Division and this had the effect of tying-in the local politicians of every stripe, and the churches too.

Within a month I was back Val was told by the Chef Constable in no uncertain terms that I was to be left where I was. Val retired shortly afterwards and I was visited by the Chief, Norman Bettison and the Home Secretary who trumpeted us as an exemplar of community policing having reduced my crime figures by more than 80%.

Once Barry, Ken and I had reduced the crime rate and had trumpeted it from every front page and local radio (I got myself a weekly slot), I had the nod from Norman the Chief that I could experiment and operationalise some of the more oddball things we could only talk about in the Community relations posts.

I chaired an active church network and went to service in a different church every Sunday. Jimmy organised coffee and cake in the Station, a fine opportunity to pick up gossip and valuable intelligence. Karl arranged training for his neighbourhood watch in speed cameras though they had no power to prosecute of course and I preferred to send warning letters though it had the desired effect. The most radical step though was to recruit local 'community volunteers.'

No place ever had enough police officers – so my idea was to make the fact that we were champions of the community more visible by adding more presence on the streets. I knew that higher community engagement translated to lower levels of crime.

*'So, you believe that people will want to spend their time accompanying your officers but without getting paid? Surely not,'* said commanders from other areas at a networking event.

I had the jackets printed with the words 'community volunteer' – and we were inundated with citizens who wanted to patrol alongside officers or record (but not prosecute) speeding drivers.

Being the Fed Rep helped of course to silence union objections and having political support was key as I managed to get a host of local people to volunteer to walk around with my beat officers, and then later with Special Constables and community support officers. I supplied them with high visibility kit, gave them basic safety training and a radio, got the force to provide insurance cover and off they went.

The effect was remarkable and very soon we had almost eradicated the minor nuisances which are a constant almost everywhere in the suburbs. I even brought my own older kids to work as volunteers on occasion and started a scheme with the local school for the GCSE kids to do their work experience with my volunteers. My idea went on to be the forerunner of similar schemes around the country.

Perhaps the most bizarre fund raising thing we did was to hold a 'Most Haunted' experiment in the station and publicise it. We got a medium in and he tried to get in touch with spirits in the old cells and various offices. I was less than convinced though it would have been lovely to have had a genuine contact.

Back at home the kids were growing up. Vicky passed her GCSEs and A levels, took a gap year in Fiji and got a place at Durham to study Sociology with a bit of funding thrown in thanks to the Army Bursary.

Ed took to rugby with Ruthin and, like Lenny before him followed the representative route as far as a trial for the Welsh national team. His claim to fame though is being picked for the North Wales team ahead of George North, later the star of the national team.

Kate was very active in school activities especially the cadet force but also the Duke of Edinburgh's award scheme and did a variety of sports.

Sarah was a problem. She wasn't a sports enthusiast and didn't feel motivated in teams. I had by this time however begun to work out the

secret of success in getting my offspring into the best universities irrespective of exam results, and playing representative sports was key. So how to help Sarah.

We searched and searched and eventually settled on fencing. There was a small club in Ruthin. Fencing has few adherents but has a decent profile at Olympic level and in the private school system.

After a not inconsiderable effort on Sarah's part (she took to it well and was genuinely good), and many, many miles attending competitions the length and breadth of Wales, Sal finally got a place in the Welsh team.

So most of my off duty time was taken up travelling the country furthering the sporting ambitions of my younger children. Fencing in Cardiff and Pembroke (of all places). Rugby just about anywhere and cadet camps around Wales. Not to mention taking Vicky to various railway stations and army camps.

In 2003 though it was my silver wedding anniversary and Pat and I decided to take advantage of Vix's gap year and visit her in Fiji as part of an 'around the world in eighty days' tour. We bought a round the world air ticket and booked our accommodation, USA, Fiji, New Zealand, Hong Kong, Singapore, Malaysia, Middle East, home.

We had a great time but only got as far as New Zealand. We were unable to go any further because of the 'SARS' pandemic and so came back again via the Cook Islands, Tahiti and the USA again. I always fancied going to the far east but have never made it, as you will see in the next chapter.

# The Road Goes Ever On and On

**'If you've 'eard the East a-callin',
you won't never 'eed naught else. No! you won't
'eed nothin' else
But them spicy garlic smells,
An' the sunshine an' the palm-trees an' the tinkly
temple-bells;'**

('Mandalay' – Rudyard Kipling)

*'Hello, I am Doctor Caparini,
you must be the Police Delegate
from Islamabad.'*

The small stooped and balding
man shook my hand but looked
rather guarded.

*'I understand that I am to take
you to see our work here.'*

*'Yes'* I said, *just to get a sense of
the sort of things you do and
chat over what problems you get
from the local Security Forces.'*

*'Well this morning I will be working at the Lady Reading Hospital
which is in the centre of the old city. When we get there please leave*

292

*things to me I will introduce you as a doctor from Islamabad, don't give any indication that you work with the Police, the people we treat are very sensitive and it may be dangerous.'*

I am in Peshawar, north-west Pakistan, and the person telling me to do this is a doctor. Peshawar is a city with close links to neighbouring Afghanistan, and the hospital where I'd been taken on a fact-finding mission treats Taliban fighters with war wounds. Today, there were men with missing limbs and others with bandaged heads and chests from bullet wounds (many of those bullets British and American). Grim stuff.

I watch as Doctor Caparini treats someone, when I feel a tug on my sleeve.

*'Doctor. This way, please. Please help my friend'*

To say no would have been to put myself at mortal risk because it may have led to direct questions as to who this foreigner was,

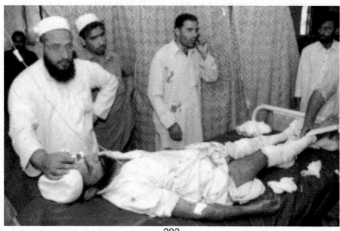

snooping about, if he wasn't a doctor. So, I followed a rather threatening gentleman along the hot, chaotic ward.

*'I need you to look at my friend, is he going to be OK?'*

What saved me was Pat. I thought of what my nursing wife would do. I looked at his notes at the end of the bed. I pulled the man's eyes down to make more of the sclera visible. I asked him to open his mouth and say, *'Ahh.'*

*'He needs iron tablets. This man is anaemic,'* I pronounced – then moved off swiftly to mimic the arrogance that is accepted and expected of a busy hospital doctor! Crisis averted!

I had spent two years at Heswall and by the end of that time the area had the best statistics in the North West of England and Wales. I had decided to take an extended holiday in Spain to use up the leave owing to me over the previous couple of years. Two weeks in though, I received a call from the Chief Constable's office to return to receive a reward as Neighbourhood of the year. This award which was a singular feather in my team's cap also spelled the end of my time in what was a perfect job. I was promoted to a post in the permanent rank of Chief Inspector which guaranteed me a better pension.

The job itself was a Superintending level post situated in the local authority offices where I was responsible for the strategic delivery of interagency services to combat crime across Wirral. I was able to mobilise things such as lighting, social services and education in support of police at crime hotspots. Once more I was managing a mixed team, this time mainly council staff who were very lazy and 'jobsworths' so it tested my skills to the limit, not always successfully

As the second half of 2005 began the countdown to my own
retirement began in earnest. I had been looking forward to
retirement for years in a sort of anticipatory, disassociated way but as
reality started to bite the prospect was worrying, even frightening. I
had spent my whole working life with the security of a Police career
about me, shielding me from the harsh realities of the job market. I
looked at jobs and the qualifications needed, and balanced it against
my age and felt that I was not suited to much else but a future in
security, a prospect that didn't appeal to me.

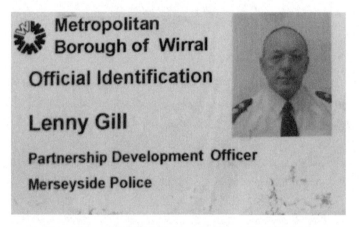

**Metropolitan Borough of Wirral**

**Official Identification**

**Lenny Gill**

**Partnership Development Officer**

**Merseyside Police**

As December arrived, I had just under thirty days left and was no
further advanced in my job hunting. Others I knew in the same
position were settling for lower paid jobs in the public sector which
would supplement their pension but they would still be working full
time for not much more than they would get on a pension. I suddenly
had a brainwave.

I thought back to all the dreams and excitement I'd wanted as a
young man. Pat and I had talked of going to Israel on a kibbutz (quite
the thing in the 1970s), of daring to travel beyond European hot

spots. That had never happened because we'd started breeding instead. My work with the ODA back in 1994 sprang to mind and I thought I would give them a call, otherwise I feared I would be pushing trolleys around a supermarket within weeks. Finding a number to ring was not easy, it took me all day and in desperation I phoned the main Whitehall switchboard.

*'Hello, can you put me through to the ODA please'*

*'Sorry there is no Department of that name sir,'*

In desperation I tried to explain my problem,

*'Oh I think this is the Department for International Development but I think you might want the International Policing Unit of the Foreign Office, I can't put you through, they have a direct number.'*

I thanked the kind lady profusely, called the number and explained my background to a very young sounding, bored female.

*'Oh, Ok thanks for your interest, send me your CV at this email address, if anything comes up we'll keep you on file.'*

Oh well I had tried and I assumed that was the last I would hear, I had played my last card.

The next day I was at a Federation meeting at the Training Centre. My phone rang.

*'Hello, Mr Gill?'*

*'It's the International Policing Unit, impressive CV, I think I have a job for you. It's in Basra.'*

I listened to the details and said I would speak to my wife and get back by the end of the day. I telephoned Lenny who was in the army by then.

*'How much are they offering,'* he said, *' Our guys are getting £1000 a day, don't take any less, you're a fat old man and they'll chop your head off,'*

I phoned them back, *'I'm sorry,'* I said, *my wife wasn't happy,*

*'OK never mind, we thought it would have suited, there isn't anything else at the moment we will bear you in mind if anything comes in.'*

So that was it. I had blown it. Two weeks later, the Christmas break was approaching, two weeks service to go. I drove to Headquarters to hand in my warrant card and arrange my retirement interview. As I drove into HQ and waited in the queue at the barrier my phone rang.

*'Hello, Mr Gill? how do you fancy Sierra Leone.'*

All I knew about Sierra Leone was that they chopped off body parts in a vicious civil war and it was in Africa. I couldn't refuse again. I bit their hand off. Lenny told his best mate in the army Tony who was a Captain with the army Training Team (IMATT) there to keep a guardian angel eye on me when I arrived so off I went.

Six weeks later I was on a hostile environment survival and combat first aid course, two weeks after that I was on a Brussels Airlines flight to Freetown. I can't deny I was frightened. But I have never been inclined to give into fear when a challenge is involved.

I was embedded in Freetown, Sierra Leone's capital. Initially part of the United Nations Assistance Mission to Sierra Leone (UNAMSIL) and after a couple of months the follow on United National Integrated Office in Sierra Leone (UNIOSIL) for which I was subsequently awarded two UN Medals.

Basically, my job was to run the Sierra Leone police training department. Sisco was the local Officer supposedly in charge – he sat at an enormous desk in an enormous office at Police HQ. I sat in that same office at my tiny table at the corner. Whenever there was a decision to be made or action to be taken, I'd say, *'What we need is this course...'* He'd ignore me of course; then, ten minutes later, he would say the same thing as if it were his idea!

Fine by me. I was being paid a full Chief Inspector's wage as well as an in country UN allowance of $1000 a month out of which I paid for accommodation, which was actually very well appointed despite the general disarray of this very poor third world nation. What I felt needed to happen did happen.

I also had an over-watch at the Police Training Centre which was a largely hopeless case despite the millions pumped into it by the UK government. Three times a week I would drive from my office in Freetown over the unmade mountain road in my big UN 4WD Nissan Trooper to the training centre in nearby Hastings, past the British army IMATT base cosily named Leicester Square and then past the Chimpanzee rescue centre.

I would go in to see the commandant, an elderly man long past caring who sat in a large empty office with no contents save a rickety desk. He had no typewriter, no electricity and no paper, just sat there

all day every day for what?  It was sad really but he counted himself
lucky he had survived the nasty little civil war with his life and all his

limbs intact. I would then look around the centre, make a note of repairs to be made and greet the staff doling out a few pence for the most needy to buy their lunch of cassava leaves and a small handful of rice. Most of the time there were no recruits to teach.

I had been in Sierra Leone maybe six months when there was an interesting incident that you may not believe but which I append a link below to confirm. The Chimpanzee reserve was on the mountain road, a tourist attraction with few tourists. The chimps were damaged, some had been abandoned pets chained up for their whole lives, some hunted and injured but saved from the pot. All without exception psychotic. The leader was a large middle aged male called Bruno. One day Bruno and three followers breached the fence of their enclosure. Rather than flee back to the wild they prepared an ambush. When the next visitors arrived, two American men in a taxi, the chimps closed the gate behind them and armed with large branches attacked the taxi, dragged the men from their vehicle after smashing the windows and disembowelled the driver and one man, the last man escaped. Unbelievable but true. Bruno and his gang terrorised the mountain road for the next three months before being killed by a British army sniper.

https://www.news24.com/News24/Killer-chimp-still-at-large-20060425

The people I met were mostly lovely, uneducated and frequently sick. On one course, one guy kept falling asleep. The delegates decided to 'punish' him by making him stand in the corner while wearing a dunce's cap. Turns out he had malaria and dysentery but never told anyone. That's the way they lived. He didn't fall asleep any more though.

After a few months I got used to the food which had been a culture shock. I got to like the Cassava leaves cooked in palm oil and heavily seasoned. There was an abundance of game fish, fresh every day. Other things were more of an acquired taste. I tasted my first rat, barbecued on a stick kebab style, it could have been rabbit except for the teeth and tail. I drew the line at monkey and chimpanzee which were captured and displayed for sale on the roadway.

The beaches were the best I have ever experienced, better than the Med, better even than the South Pacific. I spent hours on those endless deserted beaches and warm blue waters it was like paradise.

On weekends, I'd drive and explore my surroundings. As in many impoverished countries that have had sporadic overseas aid, there were haphazard improvements. I'd drive along excellent roads – that lead to nowhere. They just stopped and became tracks. On one foray, I found a deserted 'luxury' resort. I took to staying there some weekends. I was the only guest! The families of the people who used to work at the hotel when Sierra Leone was in better times lived in tin huts around the hotel. I'd give them five dollars for my stay, and they'd restart the hotel generator and catch fish for my dinner.

*'Your table is ready,'* I'd be told and enjoy the fresh catch at a table for one in the centre of a huge open dining room which would have graced the Caribbean in days gone by, a single 20-watt bulb in place above my table!

About once a month I was also required to visit one of the four outlying provinces of the county each having its own secondary training school in similarly parlous conditions. The furthest, Kenema in the far east was also the most primitive, though that had not always been the case. This was the home of the infamous 'blood diamond' industry. A visit to an open cast diamond mine was like a trip back to the days of ancient Rome. The miners were not technically slaves of

303

course but the conditions were horrific. Excavated diamonds would change hands for a few dollars and would eventually be traded for thousands on the European markets.

One day. On a drive a couple of hours east of Kenema town, I discovered what had been a small town in the days of the British, just seventy years previously, now overgrown and deserted. It was a scene from a post apocalyptic disaster movie. I peeled back thick vegetation to find red post boxes bearing the monogram GvR (King George V); a railway station now reclaimed by the jungle, deserted but still

furnished; abandoned when the tracks had been lifted and taken away by previous dictatorships because the metal was of value. Everywhere, people, desperately poor people, carrying on because what else could they do?

I had been in Sierra Leone for just a few weeks when Pat told me my mum had been taken into Hospital. She died late in February and I travelled back for her funeral. This time is really a blur, I have little recollection of my journey back, even the funeral itself was sketchy though I do remember an undercurrent of bad feeling which seemed to be related to what would now happen to Ian and our inability and frankly unwillingness to take him on. He needed to begin his own new life in sheltered care.

When I returned after just a week at home, I resumed wok. Lizzy and Sarah visited in the early summer and Len and Ed followed later in the year.

The international politics of Sierra Leone was complex. It had of course once been a British colony but had achieved independence in the 1960s.

When the civil war broke out the United Nations deployed a peace-keeping force but its effectiveness was poor. It took a short, brutal intervention by Tony Blair's government after a small unit of

British troops had been captured and tortured to pacify the country which was achieved with remarkable rapidity. The UN were sidelined but continued with their mandated mission. So my UN attachment therefore carried a disproportionate influence on the policing mission although it was headed by a much more senior officer first from India then from the USA.

One result of this influence was my relationship with the British High Commission to whom I was actually more answerable than to the UN head of mission. Part of that relationship was attendance at formal functions such as he Queen's birthday party.

I first met with a senior official from the International Committee of the Red Cross (ICRC) at that party, the gold star of international aid work. Days earlier, I'd been visited by his team and had turned down their demand to run a training course for them. Our schedule had no spaces! Eventually, we were able to accommodate the course and, when my posting ended, I was approached to work for them.

*'I understand you might be prepared to come and work for us,'* I heard in a phone call with a senior ICRC man.

*'We have booked you onto a training course in Geneva, all expenses paid. If we appoint you to a post We'll pay for your wife to accompany you. We'll also pay school fees for your children so they can board in the UK.'*

I was initially offered an accompanied post in Sri Lanka (home to 86 species of lizards, according to Google), despite the snakes and lizards which Pat hates, I convinced her. I soon found out it's not that

306

straightforward with the ICRC. Just weeks away from the planned move,

*'You know we said Sri Lanka, well now we want you to go to Dhaka.'* I thought they meant Dakar West Africa and was minded to turn them down.

*'No Dhaka Bangladesh.'*

More negotiation and the posting finally turned into Islamabad, which was then in the middle of a terrorist bombing campaign. Nonetheless we both took a deep breath and went for it. Ed who was the last one at home managed to get into Kirkham Grammar School, (a private boarding school near Blackpool with an enviable Rugby reputation), based on his outstanding performances at Welsh representative level.

So Pat and I began our Asian adventure. We lived in the ground floor flat of a detached house in the best part of Islamabad. I went to the local bazaars and bought furniture and rugs to furnish the place which I still have here in Wales, and all at remarkably reasonable prices. I was allocated my own Toyota Landcruiser and had a driver for longer journeys. When I was away on visits across Pakistan, Pat

stayed in the flat along with two guards (one a former Mujahideen fighter, the other a Pakistan Army Sergeant major), a gardener and a house boy who waited on us hand and foot, did all the washing and ironing, cleaned and made the beds, and generally acted as Major Domo. Such is the life even today of the new 'Aid Colonials' and their 'Trailing Spouses'.

When in Islamabad, apart from shopping we would go to the British Embassy Club, perhaps varying it with, say, the Canadian Embassy Club. Always, and rightly, we were cautious. One night we were woken by a huge terrorist bomb in the middle of the night. I went back to sleep. There was nothing I could do and I was safer in bed.

My job was titled 'Police and Security Force delegate' and I had to network with the said Police and security forces (not including the regular military). Pakistan is divided into five Provinces, Punjab (capital Lahore), Sindh (capital Karachi), Balochistan (capital Quetta), North West frontier (capital Peshawar) and Jammu Kashmir (capital Muzzafarabad). In addition Islamabad District is a separate entity and a number of border areas collectively known as the Federal Tribal Areas share a migratory population with Afghanistan. Each Province had at least five forces I needed to link into both Police and paramilitaries. In addition I also inked with Tribal 'Lashkars' or militias.

I was also responsible for similar networking with the National Police and armed Police in Nepal and the same in Bangladesh (the armed Police there were called the Rapid Action Battalion and had a fearsome reputation). I travelled extensively being away three days per week, more on occasion. Travel within Pakistan was too dangerous to take Pat, but she came with me to Nepal and Bangladesh. I developed close personal friendships with senior officers from many of these forces.

In the North West Frontier I travelled to Peshawar and up the Khyber pass to Afghanistan, past the largest lawless market in Pakistan which lay a few miles outside the city on the Khyber Road. It was rumoured you could buy any type of armament from Kalashnikovs to Surface to Air Missiles, even old Russian tanks in that market. While I was there I helped out during a major flooding disaster and

with the administration of the refugee camps, as well as my already
described visit to the hospital in Peshawar where we treated the
Taliban.

I was also involved in the response to a small sharp war in Swat
where the Pakistani Taliban fought the Pakistan army and captured a
sizeable area advancing to within 30 miles of Islamabad itself. One of
our delegates, an Irish citizen was 'invited for tea' a euphemism for
being kidnapped and I negotiated his release and safe conduct back to
the capital from the Taliban.

I don't think Pat has completely forgiven me for stopping her
going to visit the Taxila archeological site with the Pakistani '*Ladies
that Lunch*' due to the proximity of Taliban forces, closer at the time
than they all really knew!

In Sindh I was actually briefly arrested along with a number of colleagues who (unlike me) had failed to renew their permissions to enter the province. Another protracted negotiation this time with the Pakistani Military Intelligence (the ISI). With the help of my contacts there I managed to get them released after three days.

Balochistan was perhaps the most dangerous with an active insurgency by Balochi separatists whom I had to liaise with in the mountains east of Quetta at a time when there were frequent attacks on security forces. I arrived in Quetta on my first visit, landing at the airport and driving through the small desert city to the ICRC delegation office. I was tired from the journey and shown to my room on the first floor telling my colleagues I would have a nap for an hour.

I looked out of the window overlooking a marketplace about thirty yards away and then sat down on the edge of the bed to unlace my boots and remove my trousers. As I bent down a car bomb went off in the market and blew the window in; glass flying over my head and filling the room. I was miraculously unscathed. Another Guardian Angel intervention I think.

For a few bizarre months it seemed that wherever I went, my departure was marked by a massive explosion. I began to worry that such co-incidences might be picked up by the authorities too. Peshawar American Consulate - *boom!:* Lahore Cantonment - *boom!:* Karachi Naval base - *boom!*: Islamabad Frontier Corps camp - *boom!* Even New Delhi Connaught Place - *boom!* I felt like a Jonah.

On another trip to Quetta I went with an English colleague who was in charge of the Quetta Delegation (I think he was really a spy) to a high class hotel (the only one there) to meet with 'friends' as he described them. We walked in and joined a group of nine elderly turbaned men in traditional Afghan dress. Tea. Sweetmeats. All as cosy as you like. I wasn't sure why I was included but the old gentlemen all spoke English with varying degrees of fluency. They turned out to be the Taliban council in exile and my colleague was discussing the arrangements to evacuate and treat their wounded from the war being fought with the UK and USA less than fifty miles away across the border. Lenny too was in Afghanistan with the army. He lost a Sergeant killed by the Taliban on that tour!

I have watched the television news enough since to know that some of these men would subsequently become very famous Taliban leaders. Suddenly One of the men offered me a cup of tea and began talking to me directly as my colleague tucked into Pakistani sweets.

*'So, what is your name Sahib?'*

*'Oh, My name is Leonard.'*

*'Ah you are English too I think?'* Interested, not just being polite, *'and, do you have any children?'*

*'Yes six,'* He laughed and said something in Afghan to his colleagues.

*'Why – you could be an Afghan! That is unusual for an Englishman to have this many children no?. What do they do?'*

*'Two are in the army. A daughter in training. My son, Lenny, same as me, he's in Lashkar Gahr right now, in fact.'*

312

*'Is he?'*

A long pause. Then – a smile and an outstretched hand.

*'Leave it with us, Mr Gill. We'll pray for him and make sure no harm comes to him if it is in our power.'*

Bravado or fantasy, I know not but Len remained unharmed and returned to us in due course. Did my meeting bear a part on that? I will never know.

On a trip to a port called Gwadar which is on the Arabian Sea, my French colleague and I were the first Europeans to visit this closed city for several years.

In Kashmir I was honoured to be invited to attend a 'Jirga', which is an assembly of leaders that makes decisions by consensus according

313

to Pashtunwali, the Pashtun social code. It is conducted in order to settle disputes. In a single week I visited the Pakistani side of the line of control which is a UN enforced border between India and Pakistan, and three days later visited the opposite spot on the Indian side. A rare experience for anybody.

I mainly liaised with Pakistani police about human rights. But whilst my core goal was to teach them about the laws of armed conflict, I was wily enough to wrap it up within what they wanted to achieve. I created a pocketbook for officers that, blow by blow, told them what to do in case of emergencies, baseline instructions such as 'call the control room' first, then get into your car. It also included... the laws of armed conflict so ICRC were happy too.

I worked on a domestic abuse project. Women in Bangladesh couldn't go into a police station to report their injuries – a distant relative at the very least would always spot them. My project set about establishing safe houses where these traumatised, frightened women could go.

A final responsibility was visiting prisons to assess whether they complied with International law. On one occasion I visited the Multan prison and spent a nervous afternoon surrounded by more than fifty death row prisoners many of whom had committed brutal murders and awaited their appointment with the Hangman. Despite this, they all seemed pleased to see me, were curious and like a bunch of children in a primary school being visited by a celebrity. Not threatening at all but I never lost the feeling it could have been suddenly different if I had said the wrong thing. The meeting, in the exercise yard of baked earth was conducted in 55 degree heat and I sat there in a suit and tie. When I got back to my accommodation I spent the rest of the evening in a cold bath but got mild heat stroke nonetheless.

Pat and I also took the chance to travel to neighbouring countries Both Edward and Sarah flew out to stay with us too. Our best trip was to India via the land crossing point at the Wagah border where daily shows are held for the changing of the guard and elite troops from both countries each more than six feet six inches tall try to outdo each other in their marching skills. As we crossed the border we were the guests of the respective border guards, unfortunately in the process I stumbled and broke my toe.

We visited Nepal with Ed and I met up with Navraj who was a friend I had made on the UN team in Sierra Leone, now the Regional Commander in the Pokhara Region which is a magnet for adventure holidays. He arranged for free accommodation and access to several opportunities of a lifetime. I went on a microlight flight to the

Anapurna base camp and then took the opportunity of a paragliding flight. I got a ramshackle taxi and we wound our way ever upwards to tremendous height above the Pokhara valley.

After almost an hour's drive my driver got out and we trekked another 1500 feet along mountain paths where he eventually handed me over to a French Paragliding instructor who buckled me into a harness and attached the harness to himself via a long rope which was in turn attached to a parachute.

*'Ok, so you can see that you are all connected to me. When I tap you on the shoulder I want you to run to the edge,'* indicating a cliff edge about twenty yards away which was above a sheer cliff around two thousand feet above the valley floor; *'and simply leap off'* he went on, *'don't hold back. I will be behind and as you can see I am connected to the chute. You will drop quite quickly but don't panic.'*

I have always been frightened of heights, but I had come too far to go back now so I ran straight off the cliff and after what seemed an age of falling, just a couple of seconds really I rose on an eddy of air and soared above the valley.

We had a lovely holiday in India where we met Sarah and her boyfriend Ian, taking in the Golden Temple in Amritsar, then onto Delhi and the usual tourist spots, Red Fort, Taj Mahal and so forth. The holiday culminated in Rajasthan staying at a maharajah's palace called the Umaid Bhawan in Jodphur with palatial rooms and our own private butler. We got in at just the right time too, because the monsoon season was late that year and we arrived by chance the week after the rains should have started but held off long enough for us to stay. Because of this we negotiated a 90% reduction in the rates.

Bangladesh though was a terrible place and I was heartily glad that in the original offer of an ICRC post we had not ended up there on a permanent basis, Pakistan is so much nicer, and so are the people. I have nothing really good to say about the country, the climate is oppressive, intensely hot and damagingly humid. Poverty levels are the worst I have ever seen. There is an entire settlement in Dhaka which lies across a railway line in constant use, traders and shoppers leap out of the way when a train comes along. The traffic is almost permanently at a standstill and stationary drivers are subjected to begging by organised gangs who routinely steal or buy small children and mutilate them before sending them out to beg to garner more sympathy.

https://www.youtube.com/watch?v=7qydStYoJSI

So many people simply live their whole lives on the street. One day we saw a young girl no more than a young teenager giving birth to a baby on the sidewalk feet from our car with only a flimsy sheet of plastic to shelter in. Even the fruit sold on the street is injected with formaldehyde to preserve it and poison the punters when they eat it.

The Bangladeshi Police Training school is in a town called Rajshahi which is in the west of the country on the border of India which can be seen across the wide river Padma. I had cause to deliver a number of lectures there and travelled with an ICRC colleague Rumana. She suggested that Pat should come too and she booked us into a government hotel she said was 'really nice'.

Just travelling there was an alarming experience. The roads are crazy and I am glad we had an experienced driver. Buses and lorries play chicken on single carriageway roads with no way out except deep water filled ditches, Eventually though we got there, shaken but not

stirred! We pulled up outside a dirty colonial era building with litter and grime everywhere. As we climbed the three steps toward the reception, a panting dog and its new litter lay on the floor and we were forced around it. The dog, a small emaciated creature was feeding about seven or eight new puppies and rats were running over dog, puppies and all. With some trepidation now we went in and registered. We were directed up the stairs to a filthy room containing two single beds covered in mosquito nets which were very much needed and little else; the only light was through yellowed frosted windows on the wall behind the bed bordering the corridor. In the far corner of the room was a door bolted on the room side which led to a toilet with simply an open hole on the floor. Why a toilet would need a bolt on the outside of the door we never knew unless it was for the rats. Pat and I spent the night huddled together in one single bed, I ended up with burns on my back from the mossquito chemical on the net.

The next day I gave my lectures and thankfully accepted the hospitality of a room at the camp, officer's mess a picture of which is on the previous page, which was built in the eighteenth century by Clive of India and was both clean and well appointed. It hadn't changed since the Indian Mutiny I am certain. The commandant ordered a police officer to sleep in the floor outside the door of our room to see we were not disturbed. I thoroughly enjoyed my stay there except for the cold curry breakfast but Pat was unhappy with the wildlife.

# Close Shaves

> **'The better part of valour is discretion;**
> **in the which better part I have saved my life.'**
>
> (Sir John Falstaff, in *Henry IV, Part One*, 1596)

The constant hum of the air conditioning unit is ever present as I lie deeply asleep in my furnished container. Outside, it is stiflingly hot and humid, even at night; but inside, the room is cold. I like it that way, set always at sixteen degrees, it is a lovely contrast to the warmth of my bed as I snuggle beneath a plump quilt. Something though has disturbed me. I float into groggy consciousness and now want to pee but am too lazy to make a move just yet. Suddenly a boom. *'Boom! Boom!'* And the container shakes me into full wakefulness. I lie frozen, senses heightened and listen. Shouting now in the distance as the first greyness of dawn lightens the drawn curtains behind my head.

*'Boom! Boom!'* again and I peek out of the window to see an armoured vehicle fifty yards away beyond the fence on the unmade roadway outside our compound. The rat-tat of a Fifty Cal machine gun bursts out briefly then silence and after a few minutes the normal dawn sounds resume.

324

After two years with ICRC I thought it time for a move, time to see somewhere else. These feelings coincided with a phone call from Alan, the former head of the Metropolitan Police OSD (the TSG) who had worked with me in Sierra Leone; and Pat telling me she too had had enough and wanted to go back to the UK.

Would I be interested in a gig in Sudan which was heading towards an independence referendum? I was offered almost twice the money so I left the ICRC. Before I did though I was asked by a colleague where I was going,

*'Malakal'*, I said.

*'Oh I have been there, before coming here,* its a muddy hole in the middle of the desert.'the young Swiss-German delegate informed me. And so it was.

325

# LEONARD GILL

## Senior Adviser
## to SSPS and SPLA

Adam Smith International, for the Government of
the United Kingdom. Valid until July 2012

In Malakal I was paired with Chris, a very damaged ex Captain of
the Royal Irish Regiment of a similar age to Lenny. No-one had been
able to work with him for long and I was asked to keep him in line and
look after him emotionally while he looked after me physically. He
found us two rooms in a compound run by Seventh Day Adventists
with a generator running for almost five hours a day which was the
best we could get and a luxury in that benighted town.

Our job was to set up and run an operations and intelligence
centre in a kitted out shipping container provided by the American
government. We would speak to the senior officers of the rebel South
Sudanese militia and police and gather intelligence which we passed
on to our Embassy. Meanwhile we provided the rebel officers with
advice and mentorship. Meetings were conducted under a tree.
Always accompanied by hot sweet mint tea, in the blazing heat of the
dusty desert town which turned into a morass in the rainy season..

The nights were punctuated by gun battles in the middle distance
between tanks belonging to the regular Sudanese forces and the

'Technicals' of the Rebel militias (Toyota pick-ups equipped with Fifty Calibre heavy machine guns and shoulder mounted rocket launchers). Occasionally the fire fights would take place outside our own compound but after a surprisingly short time we ignored them and sat outside our rooms listening to music on our small CD players which at least partially drowned out the noise. I preferred the music of my youth, Abba, Motown and Queen; Chris preferred Bruce Springsteen and the Pogues.

I was classified as a Consultant, self employed and on a rotation of four weeks on and four weeks off. A flight into Juba, then another to Malakal aboard a UN light aircraft or Helicopter which was not the most reliable in the event of the balloon going up. Chris though told me he had worked out an evacuation plan for us should the worst happen.

He had stashed a two man canoe in reeds on the River Nile about two miles from our compound. We would follow half flooded ditches across the fields to the river and paddle with the current till we reached the nearest safe town about two days north.

**GOOD PLAN!**

The official evacuation plan though was really no better. In the event of an evacuation an armoured UN column would drive eight miles from their base and pick us up along with the other foreign aid workers dotted in various compounds around the town carrying us all to safety. In the event the plan was only initiated once and on that occasion they never turned up but remained in their base because the road was blocked by tanks.

327

I spent six months all told in Malakal until South Sudan gained independence and our contacts became the official Army and Police. After that I moved to the capital Juba and took up rotational residence in an air conditioned container in a safari style hotel with swimming pool. As the months went by though I got offers to do more work in the periods I was not in Sudan.

Although I had resigned my permanent post with ICRC, I remained on their 'books' and was called upon to undertake a number of assessments of security force activity for periods up to a week at a time. During these visits I met with both sides.

In Lebanon I was hosted by Hizbollah, in the Gaza Strip by Hamas and in Kurdistan by the PKK, all of course designated as terrorist

organisations. Visits to these organisations were balanced by visits to regular Police and Army units. It is a special experience working for the ICRC; able almost uniquely to pass across battle lines and negotiate with both sides of a conflict in relative safety.

These visits also allowed me to indulge my curiosity for ancient places. In Pakistan I had visited the sites of Moenjo-Daro and Taxila, in Iraq I visited Babylon, in Lebanon Baalbek and Byblos; and in Egypt the pyramids. The jewel in the crown though was a weekend visiting Jerusalem, Jaffa and the Palestinian West Bank archeological sites all courtesy of the Red Cross.

When I left Israel and Gaza I was considerably conflicted. When I was young public sympathy lay with the Israelis, latterly that sympathy has shifted somewhat to the 'oppressed' Palestinians. Tel Aviv and its associated suburbs could be in the South of France or Spain. All are clean and well ordered even swish. They are in sharp contrast to the towns of the West Bank which are dirty, shabby and chaotic. If it were only the West Bank though this could be put down to Israeli neglect but then the West Bank is typical of Arab towns across the Middle East and North Africa in my experience.

Even in the UAE and Qatar, once one leaves the business and tourist areas, squalor reigns. I was left with some understanding of why the Israelis, who are generally Europeans at heart would not want their towns and cities to descend into chaos. I witnessed though the way ordinary decent Palestinians were treated, irrespective of their religion. The Israelis routinely dehumanised the Palestinians and made no attempt to hide or excuse the fact. Whilst these two parallel worlds exist I can see not end to the conflict which has lasted longer than my own lifetime.

One job of course leads to another and once your name gets known on the 'circuit', the offers come in thick and fast. I began undertaking similar evaluation visits for various UN bodies. The first was in Bosnia where I was able to employ Lenny's wife Dragana as my official interpreter. The job involved research and interviews as usual of course, but culminated in attempting to chair a conference of Police leaders representing the various ethnic and political entities in the country. This was my first real introduction to the world of 'Real Politik'. It was impossible; even Dragana was exasperated as first one delegation, then another took offence, refused to engage or walked out. International diplomacy I found was not as easy as I thought.

Back in South Sudan as the new country was called; although I was based in Juba there was a requirement to travel to every part of the country to undertake research which would aid our interventions. The country had been divided into ten states. Malakal which I knew well by now was in Upper Nile State. Now that the country was independent our contacts were officially in control. The 'Brigadier' who had been the main militia leader in the town and essentially a warlord, now headed the 'Military Intelligence and Police Special Branch'. He was a useful contact and on at least one occasion probably saved me from a very dodgy situation.

Although the new army was now formed it was little more than a loose collection of rebel tribal units who continued their activities as uniformed bandits. One day as I travelled toward the UN base for a meeting; my driver stopped at an unofficial checkpoint who demanded our money and personal possessions. This potentially fatal encounter was alleviated only when I phoned the Brigadier who had given me his personal number and I handed the phone to the leader of the road block who visibly blanched and sent us safely on our way

apologising profusely for his mistake. He had of course been made an offer he couldn't refuse! You didn't cross the Brigadier.

Danger came in many forms of course. I was stranded on more than one occasion at isolated airfields when our arranged UN flights failed to turn up and waited in searing heat without provisions, communications or adequate shelter for the flight to arrive (hopefully). Other dangers came in the form of the wildlife. I was inches away from being bitten by a cobra on more than one occasion and at an isolated hotel my room was infested with rats for which I have always had an unreasonable terror. For three nights I had to lie in bed surrounded by a mosquito net tucked underneath the mattress as rats scrambled over the netting above me and on all sides. I was truly terrified and frankly would have preferred the gun battles.

Our team consisted of a dozen ex British soldiers, mostly ex Majors or Colonels and half a dozen retired Police officers of Chief Inspector or Superintendent rank. In early December 2013 things seemed to be settling down and we began a series of training sessions around the country in relation to the laws of war and human rights. It was an ironic intervention in light of forthcoming events. Together with Ollie a retired Lieutenant Colonel from the Light Dragoons I travelled to a large army camp near Bor in the centre of the country.

South Sudan rebel fighters.

I say army camp but it was more like a medieval gathering with a series of reed covered mud huts around camp fires. We were met by Peter Gadet the general commanding the area. He was in fact a tribal warlord. His entire brigade owed personal tribal allegiance to him. We had tea and cake and he introduced us to his command team. All terribly civilised though the man had an intensity which was unnerving.

At the end of the session General Gadet thanked us and waved us off; we drove back the dozen miles or so along dirt roads to Bor Town and the rats, and the next day flew back to Juba. Twenty Four hours

later Gadet's Brigade began the South Sudanese civil war. Less than two weeks later we were evacuated from the country.

Gadet's mutiny for that is what it was, happened in Jonglei and Upper Nile States (the North and Central regions) and was tribally based. He was from the powerful but minority Nuer tribe based in the north while the dominant Dinka majority tribe provided most of the government. It spread quickly though to the capital Juba because some Nuer regiments had been placed there to split them up and prevent a solid power block. It was these Nuer formations which launched attacks on Dinka units, one such attack having woken me up around dawn one morning after several days fighting which came ever nearer to our hotel.

On the day in question, the battle went on for several hours though further away and nearer and further away again . It sounds bizarre to record, but once I'd worked out what the noise was – and knew there was nothing I could or should do – I went back to sleep.

I was properly woken at 8.30am when my phone rang and Alan asked me to make my way to the dining room by the pool for an emergency morning meeting. The heavy weapons had gone apparently, or were now silent to be replaced by crowds of fighters passing noisily by and brandishing their weapons but largely ignoring our camp thank goodness.

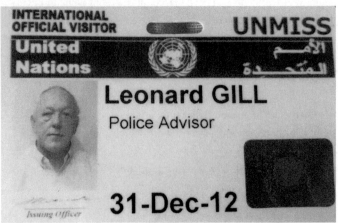

INTERNATIONAL
OFFICIAL VISITOR                    UNMISS

United                              الأمـــم
Nations                             المتّحــدة

Leonard GILL
Police Advisor

31-Dec-12

Issuing Officer

It was decided we should evacuate but the plans had not survived contact as usual and negotiations were in hand to clear a way for us to get to the airport about three miles away. Johnny, a retired Brigadier who was our senior military advisor had gone off early to make contact with his counterparts in the army brigade currently controlling our part of Juba and we awaited his results.

I don't know why but I couldn't work up the enthusiasm to panic and decided, as there was nothing I could do once I had packed a small emergency holdall, to sit by the pool and take advantage of the sun. I remember . . . carrying on as normal. I swam in the pool, listened to my CDs. The hotel was supplying us in the circumstances with free drinks and snacks. I was surprised how most of my colleagues, dissolved quickly into headless chickens who seemed to think that because I wasn't panicking I knew something they didn't. Anyway by early afternoon Johnny returned with an escort of armoured vehicles and technicals crewed by the South Sudanese military police who were a moderately elite and organised force having been the principal beneficiaries of British training and arms since independence.

We quickly abandoned the hotel, joined the convoy complete with our small emergency bags and off we went to the airport. We had to walk the last mile or so after they got us past a Government road block guarding the airport approach. I remember being a little sad to be abandoning my barrel of cider which was still mostly full and which I had brewed from local yeast and cartons of apple juice. I was relieved though to be getting out.

We had only gone a few hundred yards when we came across the first bodies. There were lots of bodies, dead from hacking and

335

stabbing mainly but some gunshot wounds or worse. The heat was intense but at least we were spared the smell inside the vehicles and everyone was giving our convoy a wide berth because of the firepower it had.

The British Embassy staff had already gone as is usual for the British Embassy staff and the airport was being controlled by US Marines who let American passport holders in first, then us, then the Europeans. The Americans refused to evacuate anyone but Americans, even the Canadian contractors working for them so our company (Adam Smith International) chartered a flight and filled up the spare seats with a variety of contractors who had become stranded.

We got out to Kenya, then I went to Dubai and stayed with my daughter Kate who worked there as a teacher for a couple of days to decompress before flying home. That was my first evacuation.

Six months later I was in Tripoli Libya, having accepted another job funded by the Foreign Office. I had only been there weeks when the balloon went up again and what became known as the second Libyan Civil War began. Two things to say about those few weeks in Tripoli, first I got to visit the enormous and pristine Roman city of Leptis Magna, a neglected archeological gem, even though the visit caused my security team a nightmare. The second was the feeling there.

I remember that there were numerous factions within the city each controlling small territories each with their own militias and road blocks. It had the oddest similarity to how Paris during the French Revolution is described in contemporary accounts. The nearest thing I think I have ever got to experiencing a city in the midst of

revolutionary turmoil. I was on the last flight out of Tripoli Airport
before it closed. In fact the shelling of the airport by one faction
started as I got out of my heavily armoured Range Rover and ran into
the terminal building. You can only imagine my relief as we took to
the air and were not hit by a missile which was a real possibility. That
was my second evacuation.

I did a few small jobs in Africa for the UN in Kenya, Somalia and
notably in Tanzania where I had a lovely few days in Zanzibar
evaluating the effectiveness of policing violence against women and
girls. I stayed at a beautiful boutique hotel on the beach and had a
splendid time. Somalia though was less fun but a lot more lucrative
and at least I could say I had survived it. Places like Somalia do
wonders for your street-cred as most people have watched the film
'Black Hawk Down'.

The UN base where I was working was hit by mortars the first day
I arrived so it was an interesting introduction to the country. I ended

337

up there writing a five year Policing strategy for them but I doubt if it was ever implemented. The big problem seemed to be that the whole country from ministers downwards were addicted to drug called Khat; a sort of amphetamine which causes manic activity and contributes to the volatility of the population. I did try some but it didn't seem to have any effect on me though maybe that is the point.

Having escaped Libya in one piece it was not long before I was contacted to do a job based in northern Syria (Aleppo was suggested) training the 'Free Syrian' Police and setting up a community safety system similar to the work I did in Wirral before I retired. The money was enormous and based on the danger: ISIS after all were on the rise and it was a proper full-on war zone. I must admit that by this time I had lost a lot of weight and was as fit as I had ever been. I had experienced war first hand and up close and was satisfied I could assess the risks dispassionately and accurately.

UNITED NATIONS

SOMALIA

**Leonard Gill**

**SSAFE Training:** 125

**Expiry Date :** 15 SEP 2018

**ID Number :** S-1827

**SSAFE CERTIFICATION**

Before the deployment actually came though, ISIS had made rapid and substantial gains and their egregious atrocities began to be made public with the horrific beheading videos in wide circulation on the internet. It was decided that I, as part of a small six person team would begin our planning in Istanbul and then split our time, in my case between Adana (a nice coastal beach resort opposite Cyprus) and Gazientep which was across the border from the ISIS capital in Raqqa.

Despite the pay I was unhappy with the project which was in essence reminiscent of the plot of the film 'Charlie Wilson's War' and really a shell operation for the CIA who are unpleasant people to work with and entirely amoral.

Senior 'Free Syrian' policemen would be brought across the border into Turkey by people smugglers funded by the US and UK (the irony was lost on them that we were paying criminal gangs to train policemen) and briefcases full of new $100 bills given to them ostensibly to pay the wages of an incipient breakaway state in return for substantial intelligence harvesting. In my view our intervention helped no-one and merely prolonged an unwinnable war.

On the positive side, Pat and I spent a couple of lovely weeks in Istanbul. We visited all the sites in this unrivalled world city and I put on weight again eating the delicacies in the Hafiz Mustafa sweet restaurants not to mention the kebabs. I had the opportunity to visit a number of ancient sites in south eastern Turkey that I would never have gone to except for this opportunity. Among the highlights was the Roman Mosaic Museum with by far the best exhibits in the world.

I appreciate risk – it's what I am paid to accommodate. But I do not chase danger. I carry an enormous first aid kit. Antibiotics. Transfusion equipment. Torch. Batteries. Spare mobile. Wind-up radio. I make myself as safe as possible.

When I was in the police, I'd designed courses on how to conduct risk assessments. In my family life, I did it all the time: no to an 18-

storey plunge ride at a Disney Park but yes to taking jumps on a horse because you are in control.

In regard to an international mission, I calculated I felt 'comfortable' if there was a 70 per cent chance that I would turn out to be safe. If it sunk to 60 per cent, likely I wouldn't go. And that, in a nutshell, is part of the reason why I stopped doing international work. As I grew older, my 'natural risk' rose higher – and the chance that I would come home safe grew lower.

In Gazientep the risk factor became excessive when ISIS were within 30 miles of the city just an hours drive away even though they were still the other side of the border. Intelligence also confirmed that ISIS  fighters were in the city and the kidnap risk for westerners had risen substantially. That was my third and last evacuation, this time back to Istanbul where I resigned from the project and returned home.

It was 2018 when the phone rang again. 'We have this job in Nigeria.'

It wasn't very long after 276 schoolgirls had been kidnapped by Boko Haram, the Islamic terrorists. I found out only when I got there that my job was more than loosely connected. Whereas I had been told I would work in the capital city, Abuja, I was sent to where the kidnapping had happened to help co-ordinate policing of refugee camps in Maiduguri where Boko Haram operated.

In order to cut costs though, the close protection I demanded was not forthcoming. They had, changed what I had signed up for and I resigned. It was just too dangerous.

During what became 11 years as an international development consultant, I had survived a good many close shaves. As I approached my sixty first birthday though the jobs seemed to be getting more dangerous and the remuneration bubble had begun to burst. So, the same job that I'd declared 'good to go' in 2012, say, would have been a 'no-go' in 2022. In short, less posts were appropriate or lucrative enough for me to take.

By 2020, there was another barrier to international travel: COVID. Pat and I sat that one out in Ruthin with our dogs, Tilly and

Nancy, surrounded by sheep and the bewildering number of wild birds enjoying the traffic free countryside. We survived again at any rate.

I will give the last word on close shaves to my constant companion who has enabled me to live to tell my tales.

**"Every time you hear a bell ring, it means that some angel's just got his wings."**
Clarence Odbody, born May 1653 (guardian angel 2nd class)

(It's a Wonderful Life, Frank Capra 1946).

# There and Back Again

> **'Every parting gives a foretaste of death, every reunion a hint of the resurrection.'**
> (Arthur Schopenhauer)

Pat has always been the healthier one. But that all changed in the time it took to flop down onto a hotel's purple easy chair and call out my name.

*'I don't feel well, Len.'*

This was Pat speaking, and at first, I was not too surprised. I looked over at her, sat in the single purple chair that you'll find in every Premier Inn room. She'd just come back from the shower, and looked tired and pale. We'd travelled across to Yorkshire from Wales and had been resting in our hotel watching 'Call the Midwife' in bed and she needed a shower to warm up. It hadn't worked, even though I thought the room was warm.

*'I'm so cold,'* she said.

346

Next day, Pat had an appointment at Sheffield General Hospital to see a specialist about periods of breathlessness which had been getting worse for some time.

She had been well when I had retired and when we had moved to Pakistan but something had caused blood clots in her system. They could even have been caused by one or more of the many international flights she had taken since I had begun working abroad.

She would argue the most likely candidate was a long haul budget flight to Pakistan which was particularly cramped. Or again the several flights we had taken around the Indian sub continent. It may've been something else entirely, who knows.

She had seemed perfectly well when Lenny married Dragana in 2007 in the Ruthin Castle Hotel. But by the time of Lizzy's wedding to Gilbie in Islay in June 2011, she was experiencing increased breathlessness

By the early autumn we went on a follow up trip to Orkney and Pat's breathlessness and fatigue were becoming severe and limiting.

Whilst we attributed her condition to a general lack of fitness, the GPs failed to properly diagnose or address her symptoms; putting them down to her age. A simple test (the D-dimer test which is a blood test that checks for, or monitors, blood-clotting problems) may have discovered the source of the problems much earlier but I have no doubt that GP budgets and an attempt to save money stopped this from happening. Or maybe I am being too charitable to the doctors in Ruthin.

Eventually a crisis had occurred while I was away; but with the help of one of Lizzy's friends who was a doctor in Withenshawe Manchester, Pat had been referred to the respiratory centre in Sheffield for assessment and put on home oxygen.

There had been talk of DVT blood clots at a previous Sheffield appointment where she needed to be taken into the hospital in a wheelchair by Lizzy while I was away – but for this appointment we went together, we'd know what was going on this time for sure.

Of course we never got to that particular appointment.

On Valentine's Day 2012, exactly 38 years to the day that Pat and I had met, my beloved wife died.

And on that very same day – she returned to life! How she did so is due to the most remarkable, important set of circumstances that has ever happened in my life, before or since.

But I jump ahead. so back into the TARDIS I go once more!

My association with First Aid has been a long one. You will recall from my earlier tales that was how I got into training in the first place, an act of desperation at the time to escape the boredom of a Bridewell Sergeant's lot. That also started a short and mildly profitable second job running courses for St John's Ambulance which ended when I moved to Yorkshire.

First Aid though, once more reared it's head when I retired. My second career which I have outlined in the last two chapters was funded at least in part by the FCO, DFiD and various UN bodies (UNDP, UNDPKO, UN Ops, UNODC); and each time that these august bodies employ a person in these days of the new god which is Health and Safety, then one must either attend variously titled training courses generally called 'surviving hostile environments' or some such; or produce a certificate that you have already attended.

Each time I went on such a course it included a substantial refresh about First Aid and because it was usually run by ex army medics this was combat first aid that I was trained in so, in the first six years of my new career I had attended four such courses and was very proficient if I do say so myself.

The first time I needed the skills was in Sierra Leone. I witnessed a bad car crash where a local woman was the victim of a hit and run on a jungle track on the way to the beach. The woman was very badly injured with a very severe bleeding injury. I was able, as a result of the training which I cannot praise highly enough to staunch the bleed, give her cardiac massage and restart her heart before bundling her into the back of my 4 x 4 and taking her to the free hospital.

I don't know who she was and never will but that intervention caused me some problems too, because AIDS was rampant in Africa at the time and as I had been covered in blood I needed to be tested when I got home and was on tenterhooks until I was given the all clear but there had been no time to do otherwise.

The next time I needed to perform the ultimate in life saving aid was with Pat.

From across the room, I took in Pat's laboured breathing as she'd told me how cold she was in this warm, heated hotel room. Then silence. She'd slumped and stopped breathing.

I jumped out of bed and checked her pulse. Nothing. I grabbed her from her chair and threw her across the room onto the floor.

CPR.

All the emergency first aid training I'd completed and refreshed during my police career had no more important test than this.

I applied short, sharp whacks to Pat's chest. I put my mouth over hers to push in oxygen and give the lungs reason to expand. I was on the floor next to Pat, and my wife's life was totally in my hands. I knew I had to summon paramedics and an ambulance. No one would hear me if I called out – so once I had got a preliminary pattern going with the CPR and resuscitation, I pulled away for the hardest 30 seconds of my life and got to the room phone and through to the reception desk,

*'Get an Ambulance my wife has had a heart attack, get up here with a defibrillator, got to go.'*

But there was no defibrillator

It took 10 minutes for paramedics to arrive at our room door. It was the longest ten minutes of my life. First came a young girl on a motorbike, then a few minutes later the ambulance crew. They told me I had done enough: they attached her to their medical emergency equipment and fitted an oxygen tube.

Pat, who was supposed to be dead, had survived!

She went with blue lights to the hospital, and I followed. I remain so grateful that I knew what to do when my wife went into cardiac arrest. As is Pat. We are not a couple given to high romance or over-the-top gestures because we know how important we are to each other without it needing to be said time and again.

Even so, now, on Valentine's Day each year, we have 'our' joke.

This year she was ten on St Valentines day 2022!

The crisis however proved ironically to be a blessing and may ultimately have saved her life in more ways than one. Because she had collapsed and required resuscitation, she jumped the queue and was admitted from A&E. There she was seen by the consultant she probably would have had to wait to see, always getting worse with a deteriorating quality of life and maybe too late, but now he referred her immediately to Papworth Hospital.

She was in Papworth for several weeks and her recovery took many months. It turned out that she had clots in both her heart and lungs. The resultant damage to her circulatory system was extensive. She underwent a high-risk, complex operation that essentially temporarily removed the heart and lungs from functioning to enable both organs to be cleared out.

At first, I was convinced Pat wasn't going to come out of it. I kept those thoughts to myself and didn't allow them to develop into feelings that might further frighten Pat or our children. It was stressful and overwhelming. I moved in with Vicky because her rugby home (she had not long moved in and was heavily pregnant with William her second) was the nearest to Cambridge. Even so, it was a two-hour daily drive to be at Pat's bedside. On one occasion I arrived and handed Pat her requested bottle of fizzy water as she claimed the hospital water tasted foul and she replied,

*'Oh thanks, you can go now I feel sleepy, see you tomorrow'*

Another evening after my visit I was so out of it I only realised I was on the wrong road when I suddenly responded to a sign telling me

I was in Lincoln over eighty miles from where I should be. I spent the downtime helping Vicky decorate her house – anything to avoid stillness and thought.

Full physical recovery took more than two years. Mentally, Pat still gets worried, understandably, lest history should repeat itself. Hence our extreme COVID caution. She eats well and tries to keep reasonably active.

During that period, which is in parts rather hazy Vicky gave birth to William and I also had to fly to Zagreb and bring Dragana (who was also heavily pregnant with Alex her second) home to Ruthin and then take her into hospital when her waters burst. All the while Pat remained in hospital recovering from her surgery.

In 2007, Lenny married Dragana in a register office ceremony in Wales. Dragana had been his interpreter when he served with the army during the Bosnian conflict. He is now a partner in an

International Risk and Security company based in the middle east. They have two children Anya (Anastasia) and Aleks (Aleksandra).

Anya has told her dad that she wants to be a police officer too. I can't speak for the force in, Bosnia, which is where the family live. But the police service here is totally removed from the one that I joined more than 40 years ago. When they were small, I had thought that perhaps at least one of mine would follow in my career footsteps. Now, I am glad they did not.

When it was Vicky's turn in 2009 she told me she wanted to get married at home. The land has served us well as a wedding venue. Vicky and Richard who she met at University in Durham, married here in a marquee attached to our stock shed in 2011 travelling to the Clocaenog church by horse drawn carriage while the villagers came out to wave and throw confetti,

Vicky eventually ended up as a Captain in the Army Educational Branch (the ETS). In 2019 she left the regular army and joined the

Army Reserves where she still serves on a full time basis as a resource planner at the rank of Major. Richard and her have four children Bella (Isabella), William, Emmy (Emelia) and Livvy (Olivia) and like Liz and Gilbie they all now live in Cheshire.

In 2011 Liz married next. Her husband Gilbie's family live on the isle of Islay in Scotland famed for its multiplicity of whisky distilleries: we had our 24-hour 'Ground Force' experience turning the village hall into a stunning reception venue when they married, all hands to the pumps. They now have two sons James and Tommy (Thomas). Lizzie works as a specialist a recruitment consultant and now lives in Cheshire about an hour away from us.

When it was her turn, Sal wanted a repeat of Vicky's wedding at home in Wales. She too had a marquee at home but this time in the middle of the next field in 2015, a vintage car was her chariot of choice. By this time I was quite the expert in father-of-the-bride speeches and thoroughly enjoyed insulting my new sons-in-law!

Ian, Sarah's husband, is an army major, and following a tour with NATO in Naples Sarah and Ian are now posted to Yorkshire with their two children, Hetty (Henrietta) and Max (Maximus). Sarah completed a nursing degree at Southampton University and is now a health visitor.

Edward was married next, to Becky in Wimborne Minster Dorset (it was her father's do after all). So it was less work and stress for me.

Ed had studied Archeology at Bournemouth University where he met Becky who was herself studying scriptwriting. When he left University he decided to stay in Dorset and after a spell with the RNLI he joined the Royal Navy where he still serves as a Lieutenant presently seconded co-incidentally to NATO in Naples where Sarah and Ian lived during their tour.

Last but certainly not least; Kate, went to Ambleside and Lancaster Universities and is an early year's teacher in the UAE where she met her husband Ahmed who is Egyptian.

Kate married Ahmed in Cyprus which was a good location for his relatives from Egypt and us Britishers. She still lives in the UAE with her husband and their twins, Norah and Zarah.

I am in awe of the happy, purposeful lives that my children have forged for themselves. There is no better accolade of parenthood than to have adult children who stand on their own feet – yet still want you in their lives.

Individually and collectively, my children and grandchildren bring me the greatest of joy.

# Back to the Door Where It Began'

> '**I pass the test,**' she said.
> '**I will diminish and go into the West**
> **and remain Galadriel.**'
> (The Fellowship of the Ring – JRR Tolkien)

This memoir has been an unexpected pleasure to write. It has given me the rare opportunity to reminisce and reflect.

Now though, as I come to the end I find it is time to judge myself, have I had a good life (so far)? How successful have I been? What have I achieved? What lessons can I pass on?, and what regrets do I have?

First on my bucket list is my lifelong obsession with horses and dogs. Influenced no doubt by Tex Tucker and his four feathers all those many years ago.

I have managed to live my life accompanied by dogs, Peggy, Lassie, Patch, Bonnie, Sophie, Thistle, Holly, Bramble, Thorn, Tilly and Nancy have given me lifetimes of love and companionship.

My flirtation with Horses has been more sporadic, the May Horses, the riding lessons, Heather in Boroughbridge, Pye and Scartine in Pateley Bridge and at last in 2014 *'way out west.'*

The relative prosperity my second career afforded me enabled me to realise a lifelong dream, to go on a real cattle drive. OK it was a bit like city slickers but I took it deadly seriously.

By 2014 Pat had been two years on the mend and she encouraged me to realise my dream and allowed me to go to America. I was working in Juba and set about getting fit. Ollie, the guy who was with me at Peter Gadet's camp you may remember had been a cavalry officer but he was also a semi professional jockey who rode for the Queen. He set me a schedule to get 'Ride Fit' and I spent almost seven months on a strict diet and exercise regime losing a considerable amount of weight and developing the muscles needed to be atop a horse all day.

I was also lucky that the next farm to my own home is owned by Tim and Jeanette who breed Appaloosa horses and teach western style riding. With them I learnt the intricacies of Cowboy skills, riding just using your legs, horse whispering and lassoing cattle.

Before I went though, in July 2013 I took Pat to Alberta and British Columbia in Canada to visit Vicky and her family who had deployed to the British Army Training Unit (BATUS) near Calgary. We travelled across the rockies, took a seaplane to Vancouver Island and went to the Calgary Stampede where I got my first taste of real cowboys and whetted my appetite for a real riding adventure. Seeing the Northern Lights above the prairie though: What a highlight!

While we were in the Pacific north west we also went to stay with Peter my old OSD partner and Nicky his wife, now settled in Portland Oregon and enjoying a second Law Enforcement career there.

And so in May 2014 off I went to Montana and a cattle drive. Pat cried off she didn't feel quite up to it despite her miraculous recovery so Vicky came with me instead, meeting me there. I had the time of my life and another bucket list experience was ticked off. The pinnacle of my horse riding aspirations.

So what else was on those early years bucket list. Foreign Travel! Well as you have read this has been extensive and I have seen things and been to places most can only dream about and now these yearnings for the far away and exotic are largely out of my system. Pat is still up for northern hemisphere trips where there are no lizards though and I haven't finished just yet. I have promised to take her to Jerusalem and Santiago de Compostela in Spain one day.

We have discovered the easy fun that is cruising, and in midsummer 2018 we experienced the midnight sun in the Baltic en-route to St

Petersburg (the most opulent place I have ever seen), calling at Norway, Denmark and Estonia.

So of course we shall go forth together again but who knows to where? And when?

I hope I will still go on my annual Rugby pilgrimage to the Stadio Olympico in Rome with my boys now that the long fingers of COVID are receding.

There are also always children to visit. In 2019 I drove to Naples to see Sarah and her family. I had intended to repeat the exercise with Edward but COVID intervened. In the spring of 2020, the disease also stopped another trip of a lifetime to South Africa. Vicky and Richard, having returned from Canada then went for two years to Johannesburg, this time courtesy of Shell, Richard's employer.

Pat and I booked a first class flight with Virgin and planned to visit the family for a couple of weeks, taking in Rorke's Drift (another bucket list dream) and then cruising back through the Indian Ocean and the Med to Venice to meet up with Len and his family from Croatia. We were due to fly in March 2020 but the night before South Africa closed its airspace because of quarantine regulations and so we never got there. But never mind I have seen enough of Africa, Safari and all and I am sure Kenyan wildlife is every bit as special as that in South Africa.

Next on my bucket list was a country life. I suppose that I always have been a country boy at heart. My formative time of course was in the almost rural environment of the Huyton Prefab, surrounded by trees and not a stones throw away from the livestock on Lord Derby's estate. As a result I always yearned to live in the countryside and as I've said more than once here, I don't like neighbours.

I was happiest in God's country and especially in Allerthorpe but the Ruthin farmhouse I have had for almost twenty three years now is pleasingly rural. To the north, the grassy Clwydian Range looms above. To the south, the sparse moorlands of the Berwyns afford an outlook wild and open enough to fill each day with a fresh perspective. I am surrounded by the sight and sound of sheep, dogs – birdsong and the happiness of seeing no other humans, whichever way I look!

Most days now, I like to work in the garden and then do something indoors. I have many hobbies to keep me busy. The most long lasting has been Genealogy which I began to have an interest in back in the early 1980s before digitised records and computers existed.

365

In those far off days genealogy involved long days journeying to record offices in obscure places, ferreting among paper indices and microfiche records and making notes with blunt pencils.

Family history is a draw because the search for more detail goes ever on. I enjoy the rigour of research, the delight in uncovering the unexpected. My efforts have now provided me with a Family Tree containing the verified details of almost 2,400 individuals and photographs of almost 950 of these. The oldest actual photo dates from the mid 1850s but I have collected some individual portraits of ancestors from several hundred years ago.

Children and family are the last enduring item on my bucket list. I was always rather lonely as a child, I wanted a large family and was blessed with my six. Family, children and grandchildren are of the utmost importance to me and a constant source of pride, yes and worry too.

I was brought up in an environment where religion was important to me. It still is for Pat who, I think has become more spiritual since her illness and the time to reflect. For me though Religion now is less important to me than in my youth but it has been replaced by a keen sense of the importance of identity, tradition and culture (of which religion is a part of course), this locates me within space and time.

Genealogy as a result helps feed this desire for identity. So too do the traditions of nation, people and family which I try to pay homage to and want to pass on to the next generations. The family now though represent a variety of faiths and cultures. None of my grandchildren can now be said to be Catholic though Lizzie's kids are the closest having at least attended a Catholic school for a while. Vicky's lot are Anglican through and through, as are Sarah's (though both my girls may still count their personal faith Catholic); Len's kids are Serbian Orthodox befitting their home in the Balkans and Kate's twins are being raised as Muslims. Edward's faith is his own I think and as yet he has no children to influence.

Folk music, Morris dancing, mummers plays and folk tradition are important and have become more so as I age. I am turning into Jack Hargreaves! (Who is he I hear you call, well look at this link to find out.)

**https://www.youtube.com/watch?v=1g1**

I still have that embedded socialism from my father which I had in my youth but I have become far more conservative with age, even reactionary but maybe we all do.

At home I grow vegetables, make jams, pickles, beetroot, wine and cider using so far as is possible our own produce and traditional skills.

It is October 31st, and the Gill family are playing 'duck apple'.

There's laughter and water everywhere as every child takes their turn – mouth open, head down, breath held and fetch as many apples from the bowl as possible.

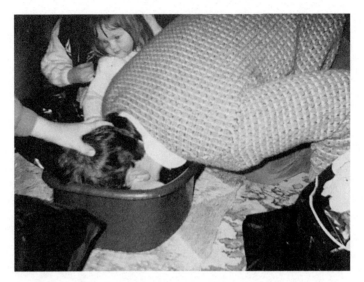

Our family enjoy being competitive, and this game is quite the Halloween tradition for us. For sure, we never ran out of apples.

Later, when the children are old enough to appreciate it, we establish the annual family cider day, when everyone helps gathering and pressing.

Was education on my bucket list when I was young?  I am really not sure but I have pursued it nonetheless though maybe more by happenstance than good judgement.

It certainly was a conscious decision not to go to University when I was eighteen.  I had frankly had enough of school and study at the time and I had bigger fish to fry.  It was also a conscious decision to re-enter the world of academia with the Open University in 1982 when I think my mind craved development  again; and what a fulfilling decision it turned out to be.

Yes the bug resulted in two Master's Degrees and a PGCE but I'm not sure it made me a better person, it just kept my mind going through a period when it needed to remain sharp and keen and it is nice from my vantage point of today that I can brag that I have these qualifications.

Recently, I realised an ambition to write a book. *'Evening of Empire: A Novel of Dark Age Britain'* (available on Amazon and Audible).

https://www.amazon.com/Evening-Empire-Novel-Dark-Britain-ebook/dp/B09MV3F284/ref=tmm_kin_swatch_o?_encoding=UTF8&qid=&sr=

It is a cracking tale of a third century 'me' in Roman Britain. This law enforcer character lives through the fall of the empire and the subsequent descent into the barbarity of Anglo-Saxon Wales. He has a large family, gets into a few adventures, keeps his moral head whilst others lose theirs. What is there not to love!

https://www.audible.co.uk/pd/B09ZPGNVBF qid=1651880011&sr=1-1&ref=a_search_c3_lProduct_1_1&pf_rd_p=c6c3 16b8-14da-418d-8f91- b3cad83c5183&pf_rd_r=SX9VCWQQK93AYYXTPGBC

This period of history has fascinated me since my years as a schoolboy at SFX. It's how transition and decline is handled that draws me to this time. And the mystery of it all.

When I began, I said I viewed myself as a fortunate man. And, I do. At 65, I have good health and a family that I love deeply. I am financially secure, have an excellent house and can look out from my log cabin office in the garden onto a beautiful natural landscape.

Am I still the Liverpool altar boy from a council estate at heart, the one who watched cowboys on a black and white TV set and knew the penny catechism and the mass in Latin but didn't have a library book in the house?

**Well; Yes and No.**

371

I prefer folk music now. I haven't worshipped inside a Catholic church in years. But my childhood values – of loyalty, resilience and standing up for the vulnerable – have steered me through life. Just as they did my parents and their parents before them I think.

I think that I have added a strong sense of purpose to the Gill family dynamic. And see that passed on to my children as they make strong and sometimes difficult decisions and follow them through.

I haven't written this book just for my grandchildren – truth be told, I want to share my story for its own sake, without pushing it onto anybody. But! To my grandchildren! I do want to say this:

If you don't learn from those in your family that have gone before, you have to start from scratch, generation after generation. And that sounds like madness to me!

So, I do have the hope that you will be able to draw something from my experiences and errors. I don't mean that you would want to do as I did. (For me, being a policeman was the best job in the world.) But what I mean is, be aware of your roots and what life has taught those who have gone before you.

I have some regrets that I didn't spend enough time with my Nan, Mrs Gill when she was old and alone after my Grandad died. I didn't see that she was lonely once she was widowed. I didn't get to hear her stories, of how her earlier life had been and what she had found out about people and things that really matter. That opportunity is gone now.

So, as Tolkien's Lady Galadriel says. 'Have I passed the test?'
The test of a successful life. Yes I have, in my eyes at least, though
you can now better judge for yourself. I think I have on balance been
faithful to my goals and persisted in their achievement.

And so I will diminish and go into the west in the fullness of time
but I trust it will be many years yet and many more adventures before
we meet at the Grey Havens and I set forth across the sundering sea.

As well as a pictorial and written record, let's make this book a
starting point for many more satisfying times across the years that lie
ahead.

**THE END**

Printed in Great Britain
by Amazon

24852451R00215